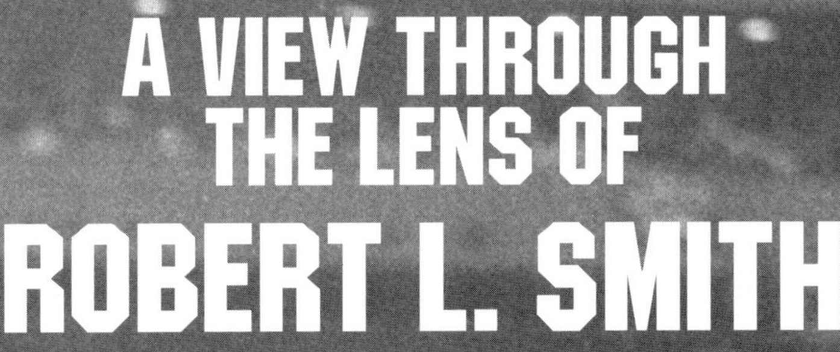

PHOTOS
1960-1995

Bob and Grandson Hunter photo by Grandma Jeanne

In 1995, our youngest grandchild Hunter was born with Cystic Fibrosis. A percentage from the sale of this book is being donated to the Cystic Fibrosis Foundation to assist their research towards a cure for this disease.

On behalf of Mr. Ralph Wilson, owner of the Buffalo Bills, an equal percentage from the sale of this book is being donated to The Buffalo Bills Youth Foundation to further their good work.

Thank you for helping us help the children. They are the hope and future of this world.

—Robert L. Smith

FRONT COVER PHOTO and FIRST SPREAD: "Football Ballet"—Paul Costa #82 makes a spectacular catch of a Jack Kemp pass in Boston. One of Bob Smith's most popular photos, winner of several state and local awards for 1965.

This book was published and printed in Buffalo, NY.

This book is distributed by:
Western New York Wares Inc.
P.O. Box 733 Ellicott Station
Buffalo, N.Y. 14205

ISBN: 1-879201-17-8

This book is the culmination of my years as the Photographer for the Buffalo Bills Football Team. My tenure started in early 1960 when I was asked by Chuck Burr, the first public relations director, to do the press photos for the team. What you see on these pages is my life's work with this team. My gratitude goes out to Mr. Ralph Wilson, the president and sole owner of the Bills, who has been kind enough to let me stay on as the team's photographer for all these many years. There was a span of years from the '60s to the '80s when I traveled with the team on their plane and lived with them on the road; for this I again say thank you to a great organization.

With these photographs I am going to take you on a roller coaster ride that will hit many heights, dips, curves, and peaks and finally climb right back up to the top to reach for the Golden Ring, better known as a Super Bowl win.

So climb on board....Let's get started....It's quite a ride....

— Robert L. Smith

Following the Buffalo Bills the last three and a half or so decades has been a mission involving both pleasure and pain. You needn't be briefed excessively on what has caused the pain. It has been those seasons when the team has lost more games than it has won.

Bob Smith knows the agony of defeat as well as I do. He also knows the rapture that comes from four straight Super Bowl experiences and assorted other titles.

Bob started gathering his pictorial history of the Bills in our first year of operation, 1960.

He is gathering to this day. He began with us at War Memorial Stadium and moved with us to Orchard Park, putting together an incredible number of pictures which tell the story of the Bills through all their years as a sports entity.

Actually, the Bills were only a labor of love for Bob. His primary job was shooting pictures for The Buffalo News, for which he tilled an oar for more than thirty-nine years.

During this time, he and his wife, Jeanne, raised six children, who produced seven grandchildren. And through all this proliferation, he kept shooting pictures of the Bills.

Was the man in a rut ? I'm glad he didn't feel so, because the pictures contained in this volume provide enjoyment and touches of nostalgia I wouldn't trade, even for a first round draft choice.

Over all these many years, Bob was always taking pictures, not only for the newspaper or commercially, but he shot many photos of people at the stadium and then sent the photos to the individuals for their enjoyment.

Bob is a great guy and I thank him for all the efforts he made over the years to record a photographic history of the Bills, which I am sure you will enjoy.

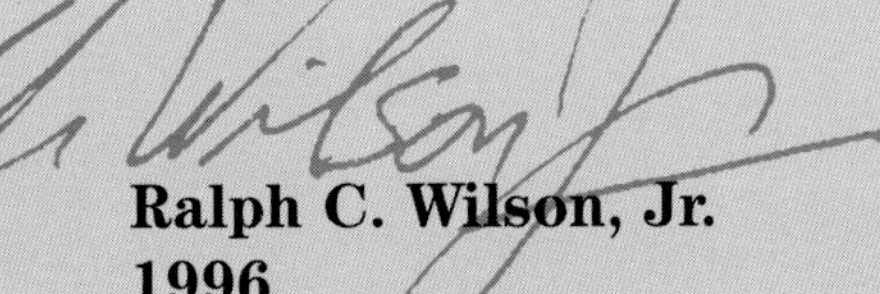

Ralph C. Wilson, Jr.
1996
Owner
The Buffalo Bills

Bob Kalsu wore #61 for the Bills. These are a few action photos of him during his stay with the Bills during the 1968 season.

1st. Lt. James Robert (Bob) Kalsu was killed in action in 1970, the only pro football player of the American or National Football Leagues killed in Viet Nam. He was an offensive guard from the University of Oklahoma and a member of the Buffalo Bills in the 1968 American Football League. A memorial plaque is on display in the entrance to the administration offices in Orchard Park, New York.

The Vietnam Memorial in Washington, D.C., where his name is etched for generations of Americans to view.

DEDICATION

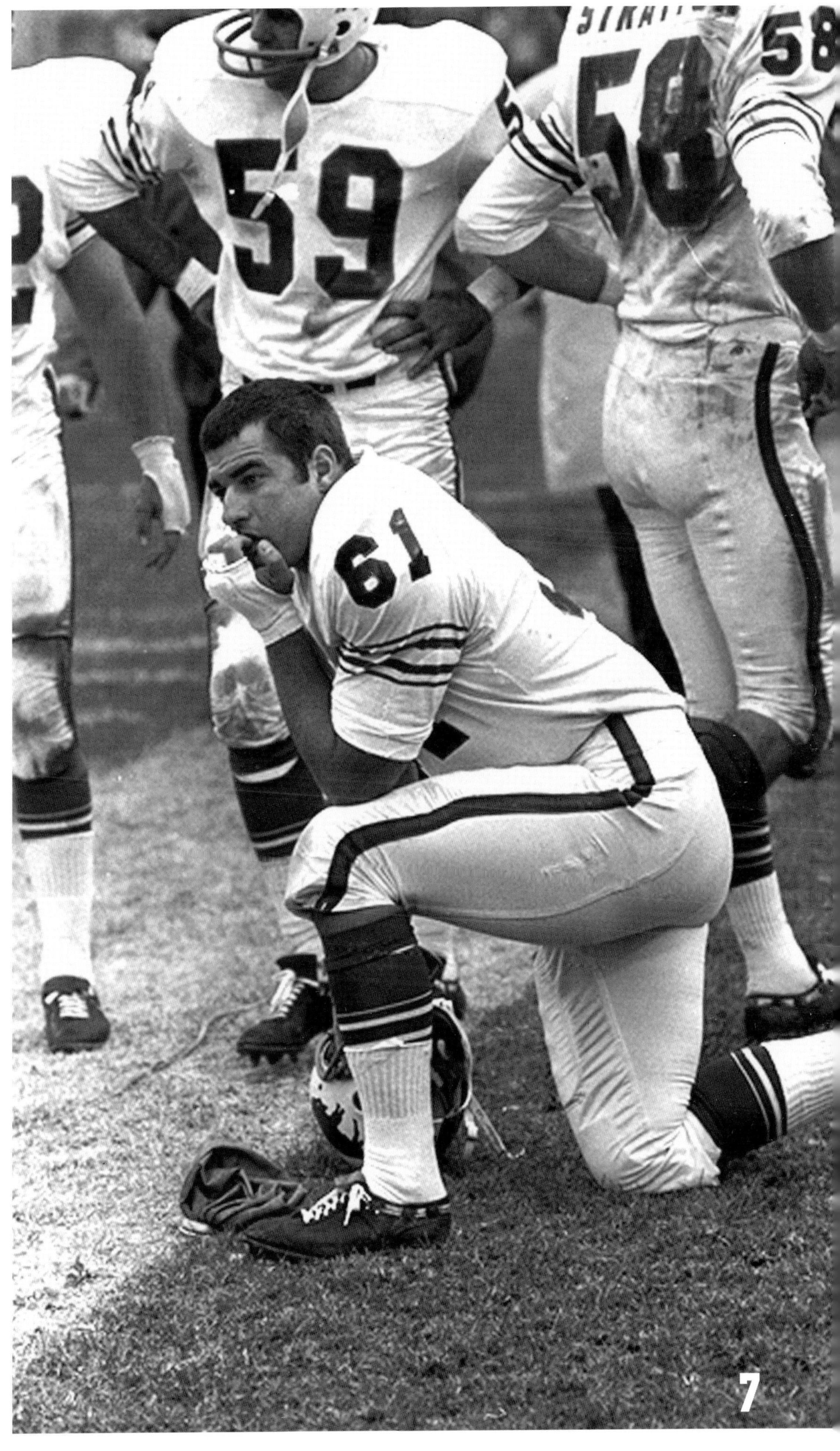

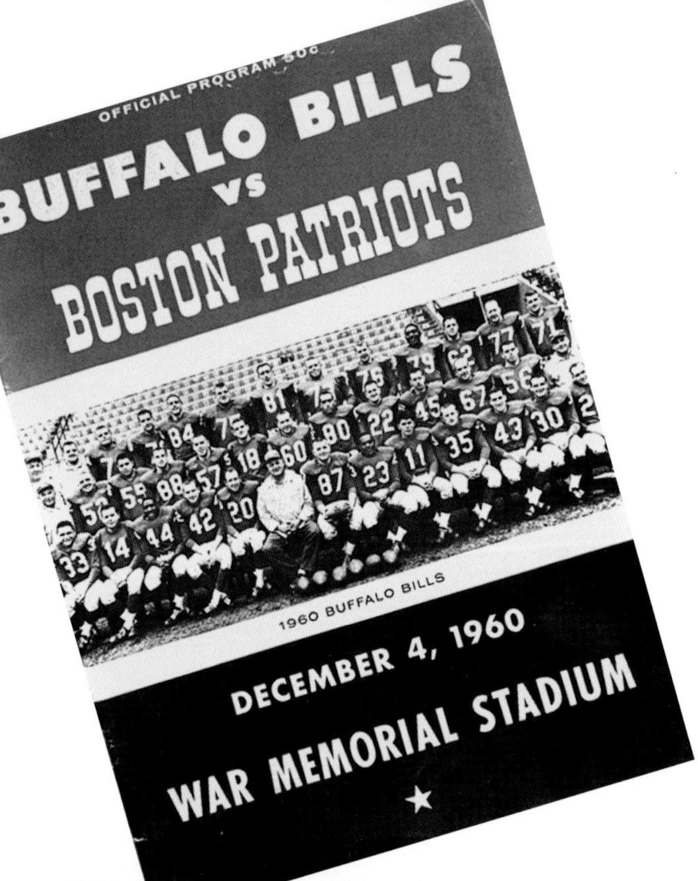

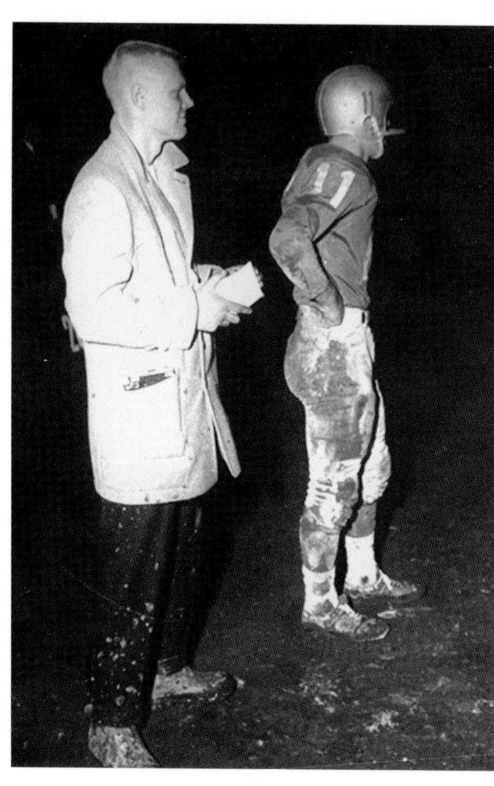

Ron Smith mingles right in with the players (unheard of today). He was a caption writer for the photographers...standing next to Richie Lucas #11 during a mud game at War Memorial Stadium.

The 1960 Team photo. Head Coach Buster Ramsey in center.

Player Joe Schaffer #67 confers with Billy Shaw, who will sign with the Bills in 1961.

*The **roller coaster ride** was about to begin....and we were all on board!*

Our Buffalo Bills were born and we started training camp in East Aurora with our first head coach, Buster Ramsey.

The top draft choice was Richie Lucas, a quarterback from Penn State. Also on board for the first training camp was Eddie Abramoski, the trainer (right up to 1996). Chuck Burr from the State University of New York at Buffalo was hired as the Public Relations Director. Players on hand were Elbert Dubenion, Lavern Torczon, Wray Carlton, Tommy O'Connell, Johnny Green, Archie Matsos, Richie McCabe, along with many others. We played at War Memorial Stadium in Buffalo, New York. The season ended with the Bills winning 5, losing 8, and tying 1. The **coaster** was about to pick up speed.

Left to right: Tommy O'Connell, Richie Lucas, and Don Chelf pose for a photo that will be used in a clothing store they opened in Buffalo that is still in business on Main St. near the University of Buffalo.

Monte Crockett #80 poses for publicity photos.

Wilmer Flowers #23, one of our first running backs, goes for a first down in the mud.

Johnny Green #18, one of our quarterbacks in the pack.

Archie Matsos #56 and Jim Wagstaff #22...off the field in a not-too-well attended game.

Wray Carlton #30, running back, posing for press photos.

Two of the coaches (left to right): Harvey Johnson and Buster Ramsey. Ramsey is the head coach and Johnson will soon become the head coach.

1960

Richie Lucas #11, our first draft pick...on the Bills bench.

The coaches group: Buster Ramsey, and Harvey Johnson kneel in front; Breezy Reid, Bob Dove, and Tommy O'Connell are standing.

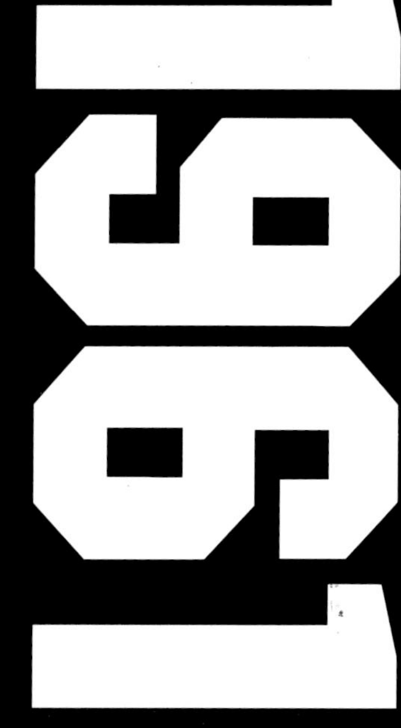

The year started out with the drafting of Al Bemiller, Ken Rice, Stew Barber, Glen Bass, Art Baker, and quarterbacks Warren Rabb and M.C. Reynolds. We ended the year with 8 wins and 6 losses, also losing our #1 draft choice of 1960, Richie Lucas, to the U.S. Army. Also on board that year was Tony Marchitte, our equipment manager, who stayed with the Bills until his death in 1979. Coach Buster Ramsey remained our head coach, but Lou Saban was already in the organization as director of player personnel. Patrick J. McGroder was hired for the front office. The roller coaster was gaining a bit of speed and was on the way up.

Elbert Dubenion #44 was known as "Golden Wheels." And here he is turning on the steam.

M.C. Reynolds #14 gives it his all for press photos.

Ralph Felton #57 works over the bag in summer camp on the Knox estate in East Aurora.

Al Bemiller attended his first camp and became the Bills' starting center wearing the #50. He still lives in the Buffalo area.

Billy Shaw #66 started. His name is now on the Wall of Fame in Orchard Park, NY.

Warren Rabb #17, our QB, at camp in East Aurora.

Tom "Tippy" Day #78 celebrated his first year with the team. He also still lives in the Buffalo area.

Stew Barber #64 eventually became the General Manager of the Bills.

Art Baker #33, a powerful runner, shows off his talents.

1961

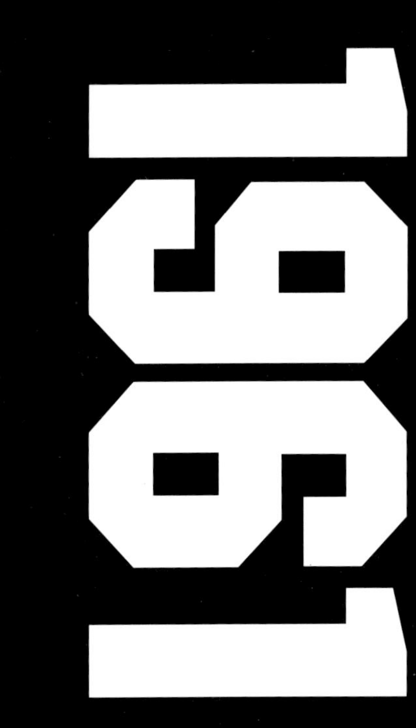

The 1961 Buffalo Bills...
Coach Ramsey in center.

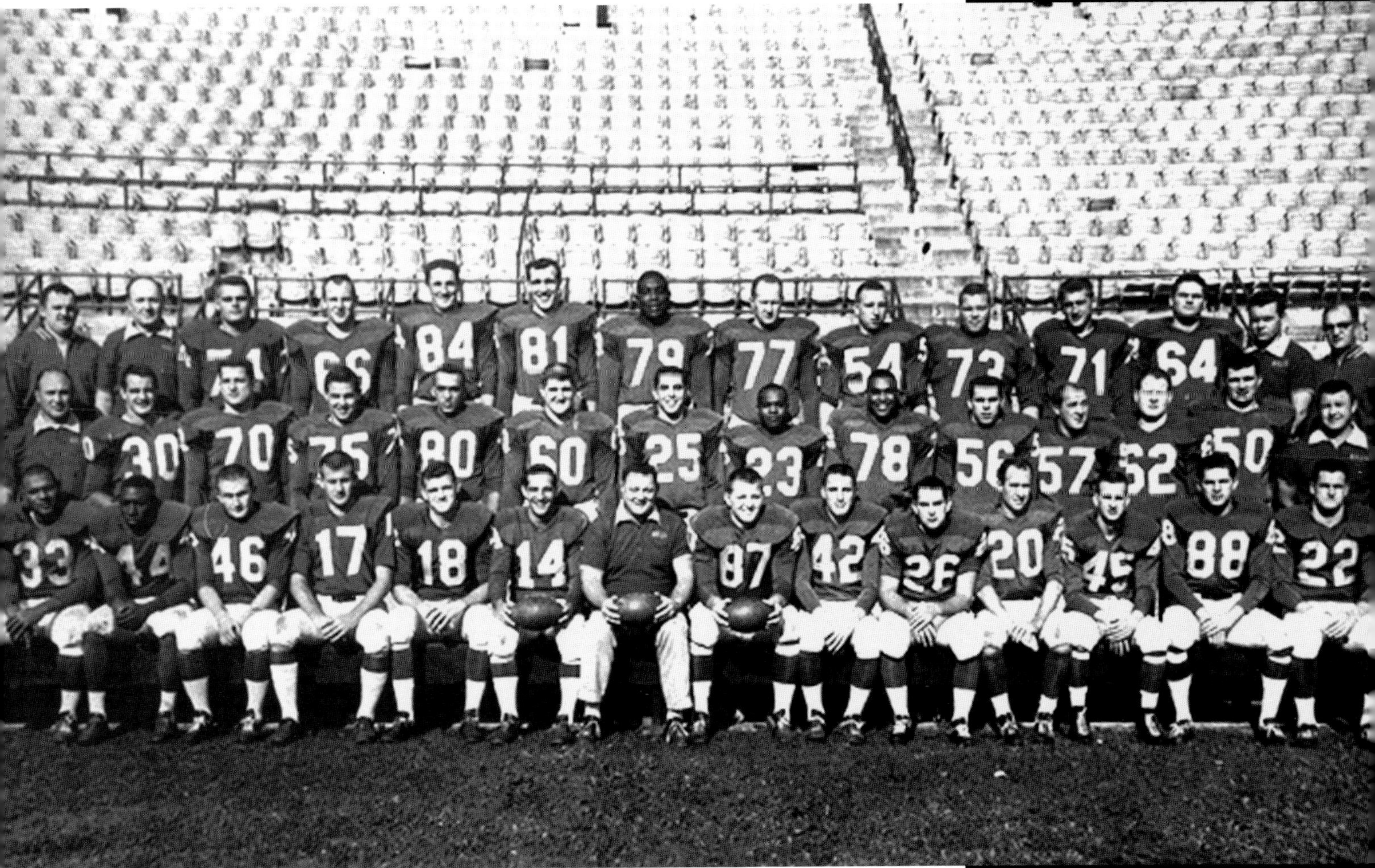

1962

Our **roller coaster** climb started with the firing of Coach Ramsey and the hiring of Lou Saban as our Head Coach. New players who came on board were Tom Sestak, Wayne Crow, and Canadian Football players Ernie Warlick and Cookie Gilchrist, who left their league to become Buffalo Bills. We traded our kicker Billy Atkins to get quarterback John Green. The biggest acquisition of the decade was our getting the rights to Jack Kemp from the San Diego Chargers in a mix-up on the waiver wires. Jack went on to become another member of our prestigious Wall of Fame. After his playing days, he became a politician in Buffalo and then on to Washington, D.C. The **coaster** took a turn and we only won 7 and lost 6 with 1 tie, but this gave us a good start toward the first peak on the ride that never ends.

This photo was titled "A Muddle in the Huddle" and was taken for an article in Argosy *magazine. The players were all standing on barrels and I was lying on the ground. It doesn't take much to imagine what the players were "threatening" to do to me as I lay helpless below them. The article was written by QB Al Dorrow, #12 at bottom of photo.*

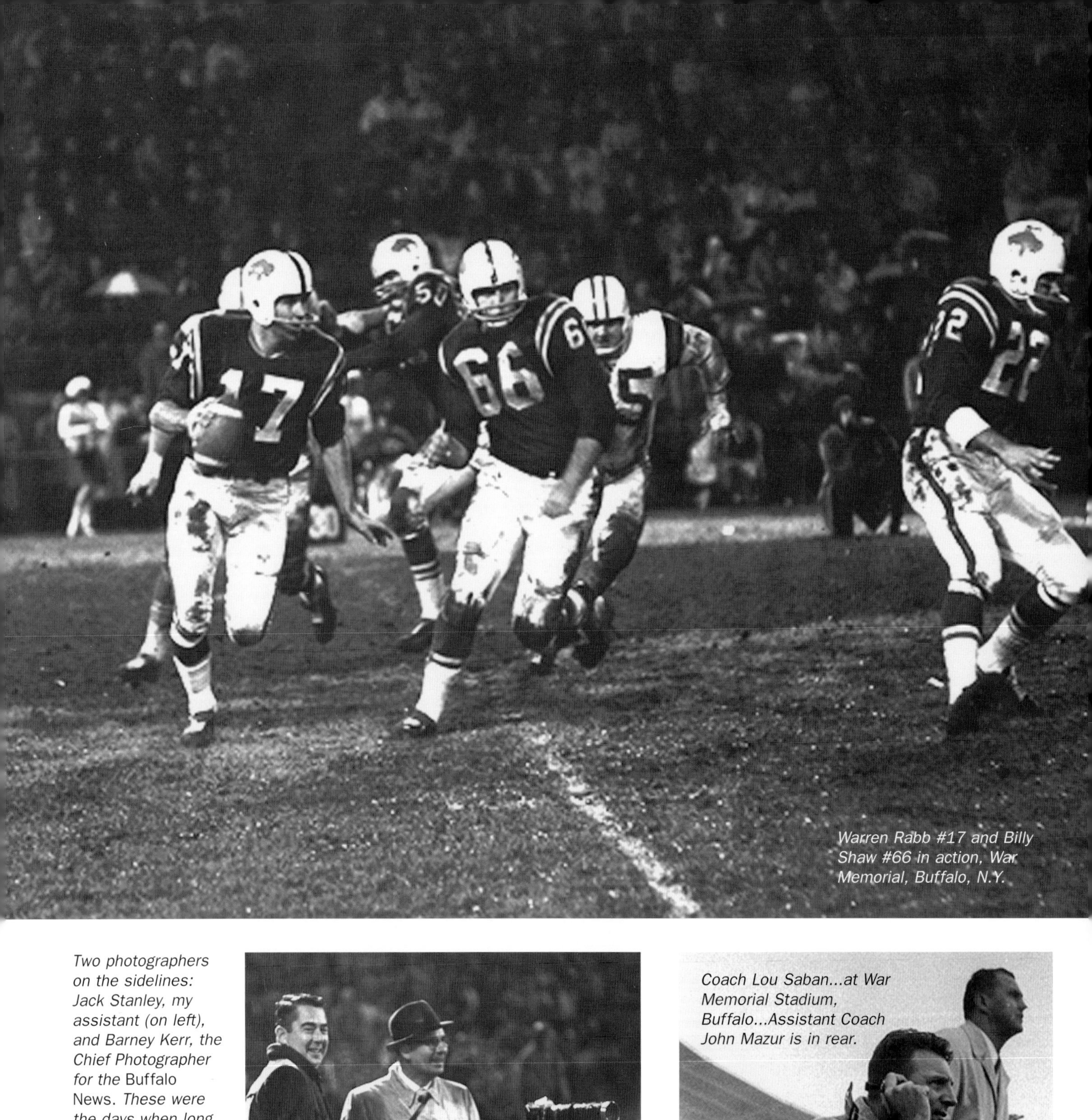

Warren Rabb #17 and Billy Shaw #66 in action, War Memorial, Buffalo, N.Y.

Two photographers on the sidelines: Jack Stanley, my assistant (on left), and Barney Kerr, the Chief Photographer for the Buffalo News. *These were the days when long lenses (not long by today's standards) were all on tripods.*

Coach Lou Saban...at War Memorial Stadium, Buffalo...Assistant Coach John Mazur is in rear.

A study of intensity on the sidelines as Warren Rabb #17, Elbert Dubenion #44, and Jack Kemp #15 watch the field of action.

One of the mud games at War Memorial. Warren Rabb #17 and Wray Carlton #30 await their return to action.

The Buffalo Jills are born...their first team.

Players on the sidelines with my Dad, Tex Smith, in the rear listening to a Billy Shaw #66 conversation.

A dressing room chat after a win with (left to right): Elbert Dubenion; Owner, Ralph Wilson; and Coach Saban.

Cookie Gilchrist #34 as we played the Patriots in War Memorial Stadium.

A typical pose for the press releases...Left to right: Al Dorrow #12, Cookie Gilchrist #34, and Wray Carlton #30.

1962

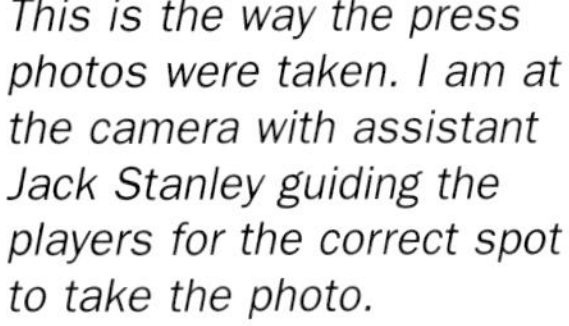

This is the way the press photos were taken. I am at the camera with assistant Jack Stanley guiding the players for the correct spot to take the photo.

Wayne Crow #22, running back...in action

In the early years, sideline spectators were able to mingle with the players during a game. This is Frank Bova of Lancaster, N.Y., who was assisting on the field, speaking to Tom Sestak and Archie Matsos.

Kicker Mack Yoho #82 on the bench during a game in War Memorial Stadium.

1963

Ed Rutkowski #40, our all-around player, as he catches a vital pass against the Chargers. He stayed in Western New York and was later elected Erie County Executive.

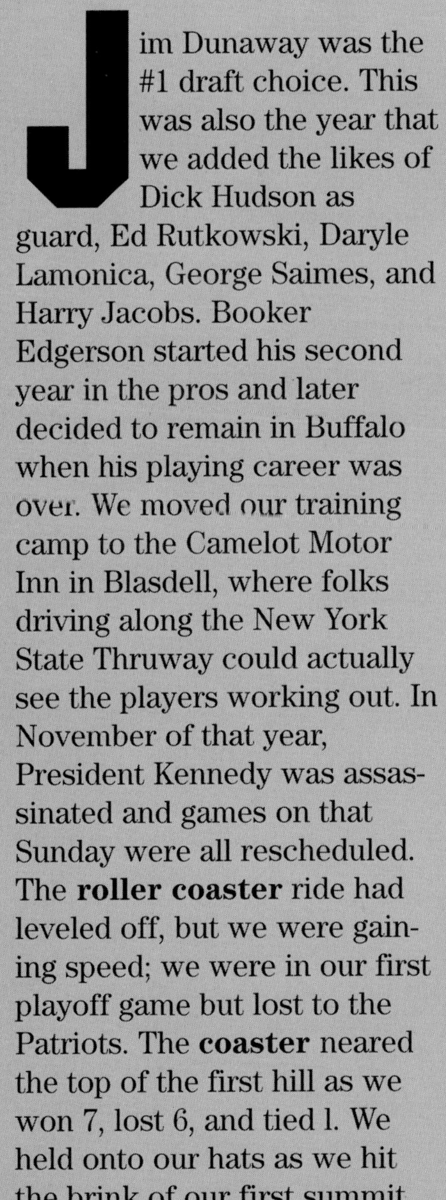

Jim Dunaway was the #1 draft choice. This was also the year that we added the likes of Dick Hudson as guard, Ed Rutkowski, Daryle Lamonica, George Saimes, and Harry Jacobs. Booker Edgerson started his second year in the pros and later decided to remain in Buffalo when his playing career was over. We moved our training camp to the Camelot Motor Inn in Blasdell, where folks driving along the New York State Thruway could actually see the players working out. In November of that year, President Kennedy was assassinated and games on that Sunday were all rescheduled. The **roller coaster** ride had leveled off, but we were gaining speed; we were in our first playoff game but lost to the Patriots. The **coaster** neared the top of the first hill as we won 7, lost 6, and tied 1. We held onto our hats as we hit the brink of our first summit.

Ron McDole #72 on the bench during a game.

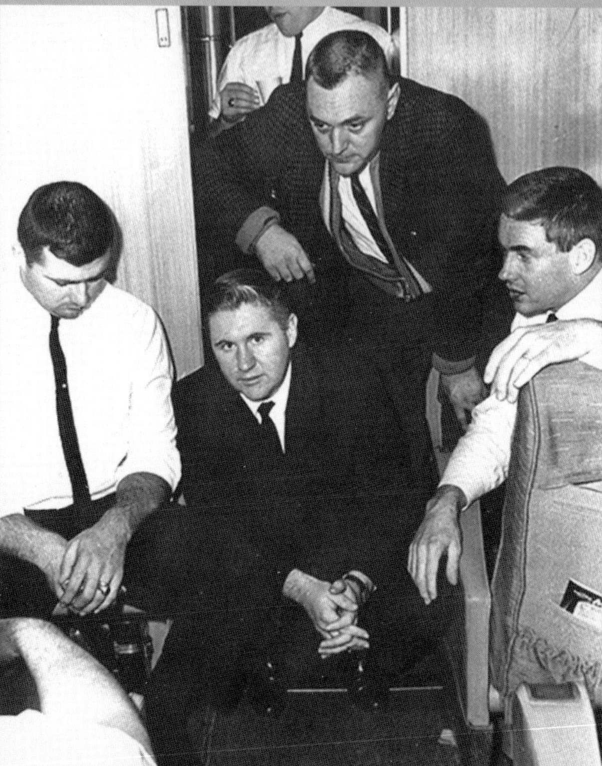

Squatting on the floor of the plane is Larry Felser, a reporter for the Buffalo News *(now the sports editor); on the left is Al Bemiller #50 and on right Jack Kemp #15. Standing in rear is yours truly. We were on a flight back from the West Coast.*

A tense moment on the bench at War Memorial. Left to right: Daryle Lamonica #12, Elbert Dubenion #44, Cookie Gilchrist #34, and Tom Day #88.

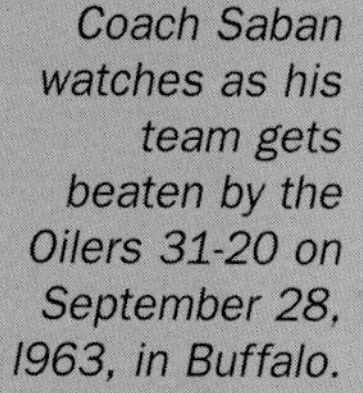

Coach Saban watches as his team gets beaten by the Oilers 31-20 on September 28, 1963, in Buffalo.

1963

It was standing room only at War Memorial as we played the Chargers. We lost this game but still managed to make the playoffs against the Patriots.

A scene in the dressing room during half time as Mack Yoho #82, our kicker, talks with another player resting.

Elbert Dubenion #44 with a reception for a TD in War Memorial Stadium.

Ernie Warlick #84 makes one of his great catches in the "old rock pile" (War Memorial Stadium).

Daryle Lamonica #12 and Coach Lou Saban on the sidelines.

Boston, MA supplies the snowy background.

1964

The **roller coaster** reached the very top—this was the year we won the American Football League Championship. This was also the year we signed Pete Gogalak, a 12th rounder, to become our field goal kicker. He was the first soccer-style kicker in the league. Paul Maguire also joined the team, and along the way we won 9 straight games before losing to the Patriots. Daryle Lamonica led the Bills to a final victory over Denver, and then Jack Kemp took the lead as we won the AFL East Division title by beating the Patriots in Boston. The exciting coaster ride went even farther up as we won our first AFL Championship in Buffalo by beating the San Diego Chargers 20-7 with "a tackle heard 'round the world." Coach Saban was named AFL Coach of the Year. What a ride as we won 12 and lost 2.

A tense time on the Bills bench as (left to right) equipment manager Tony Marchitte, trainer Ed Abramoski,and #40 Ed Rutkowski watch. In Boston, ready to win Championship.

Bill Groman #81 gets the standard welcome on the Bills bench after he scored against the Patriots.

Ralph Wilson on one of his rare ventures to the sidelines during a game.

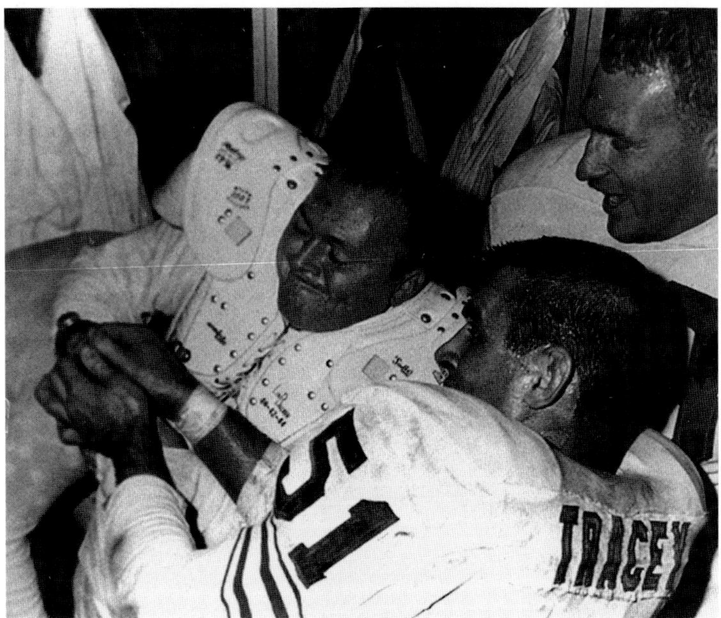

Bills win AFL Title and celebrate in Boston. Left to right: Paul Maguire, John Tracy, and Mike Stratton pop the bubbly.

Jack Kemp #15 in action vs. the Chargers for Championship.

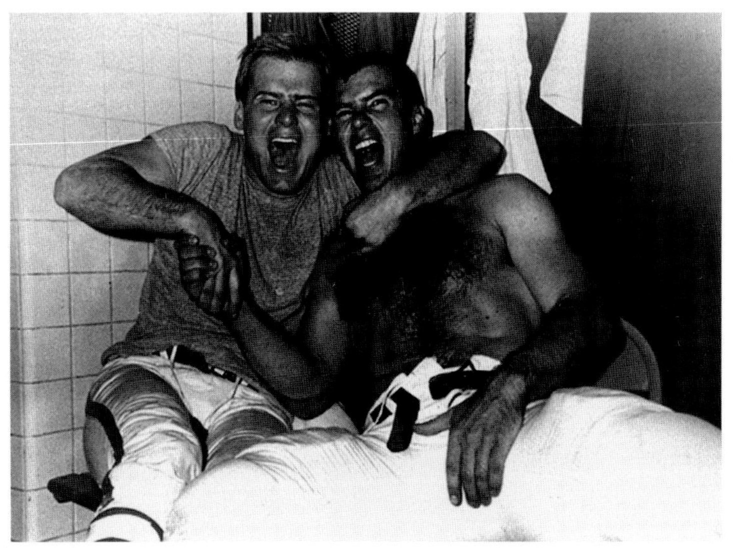
Bills win AFL Title in Boston. Pete Gogolak and Daryle Lamonica celebrate.

1964

Pete Gogolak #3 on the bench...a kicker's life is very lonely.

THE TACKLE HEARD 'ROUND THE WORLD. *Mike Stratton #58 tackles Keith Lincoln #22 of the Chargers in Buffalo and causes Lincoln to leave the game with injuries. He was their top runner. The Bills went on to win the AFL title with a 20-7 score.*

1964

Jack Kemp #15 in action vs. the Chargers for the AFL Championship.

Ron McDole #72 in action vs. the Chargers in the Championship game.

In dressing room after championship game (left to right): Coach Saban, Pete Gogolak, Jack Kemp, Wray Carlton.

1964

Coach Saban with his son on the sidelines waiting for the last few seconds of game. Ed Rutkowski is on his right.

Jack Kemp is mobbed on his way to dressing room...We Are the Champs! Top of the World!

Ron McDole #72 gets an interception against the Broncos in Denver, Colorado.

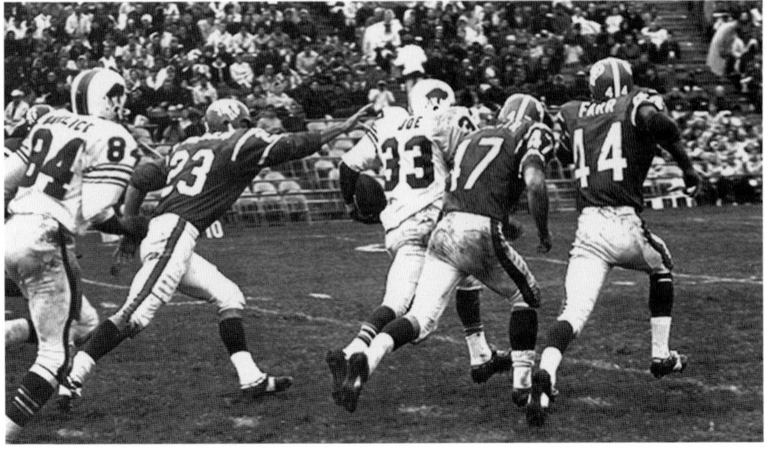

Billy Joe #33 scores on a pass from Jack Kemp in Denver.

Elbert Dubenion #44 gets the step on an opposing player in War Memorial Stadium vs. Patriots.

Jack Kemp #15 on left with Daryle Lamonica #12. Jack went on to become a U.S. Congressman and the Republican Party's Vice Presidential nominee in 1996.

Wow. ..what a ride! The Bills were still at the top of the world this year, winning 10, losing 3, and tying 1. The East Division title was won by late November, and then the Championship game was won in San Diego on December 26. What a Christmas present! The **roller coaster** flew along at the very top. During the year we traded Cookie Gilchrist for Billy Joe. A new team was born called the Miami Dolphins. Another player who was to become a household name, Joe Namath, joined the New York Jets, and became a frequent —if unwelcome— visitor to the Rock Pile. Season ticket sales soared to 26,000. Another new name that emerged was Bo Roberson, a receiver acquired from the Raiders. The **coaster** was poised at the top and headed down, but we still had 1966 to enjoy the view.

Believe It or Not ... a man from space? No, it's the Rocket Man from Bell Aircraft as he flies around the field at half time.

One of the first NBC TV cameras with the cage around them to protect them from flying objects. Bills bench is in foreground.

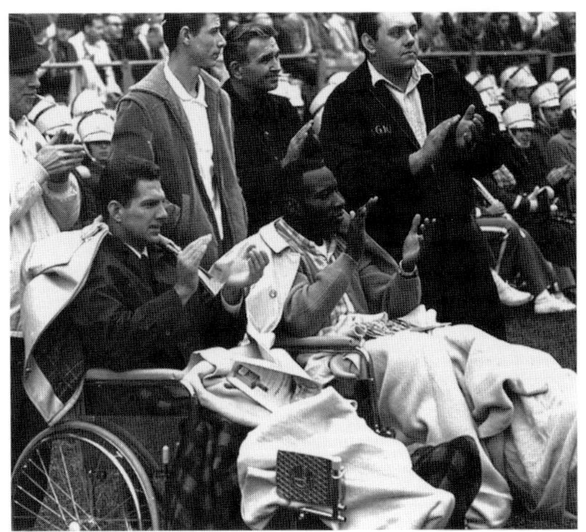

Glen Bass and Elbert Dubenion on the sidelines in wheelchairs after injuries. At War Memorial Stadium.

Joe Namath #12 gets his pro start in Buffalo as Harry Jacobs #64 of Bills chases him. Bills won 33-21.

Daryle Lamonica #12 vs. Houston Oilers...we lose this one 19-17.

1965

Pete Gogolak in street clothes goes to visit his brother Charley in Boston, kicking for Princeton. Charley went on to become an NFL placekicker for the Redskins and the Patriots.

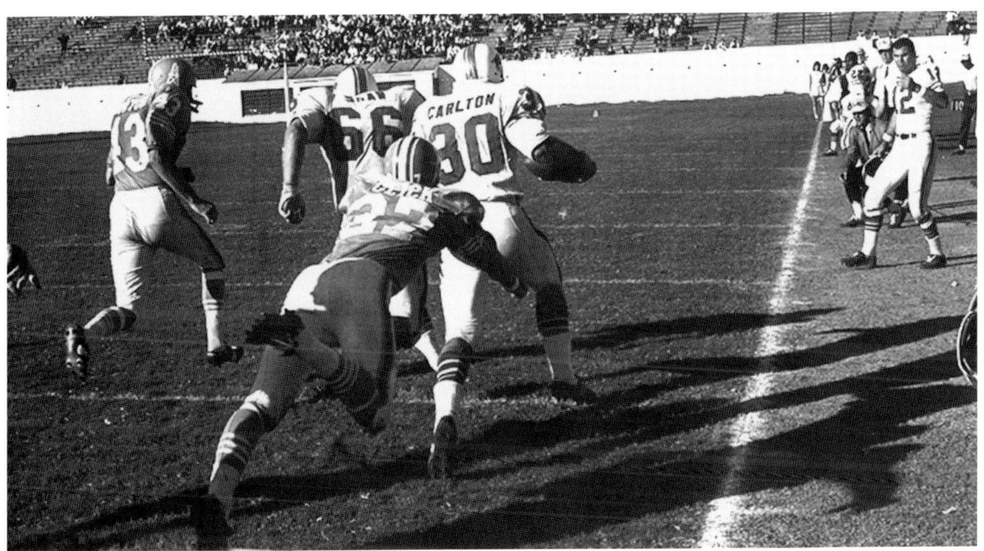

80-yard TD run by Wray Carlton #30 in Buffalo as we defeat the Oilers 29-18. Leading the way for Carlton is Billy Shaw #66.

A tired and beat Tom Sestak #70 returns to the Buffalo bench.

Ron McDole #72 has a fine day against the newcomers (Dolphins) as we win 58-24.

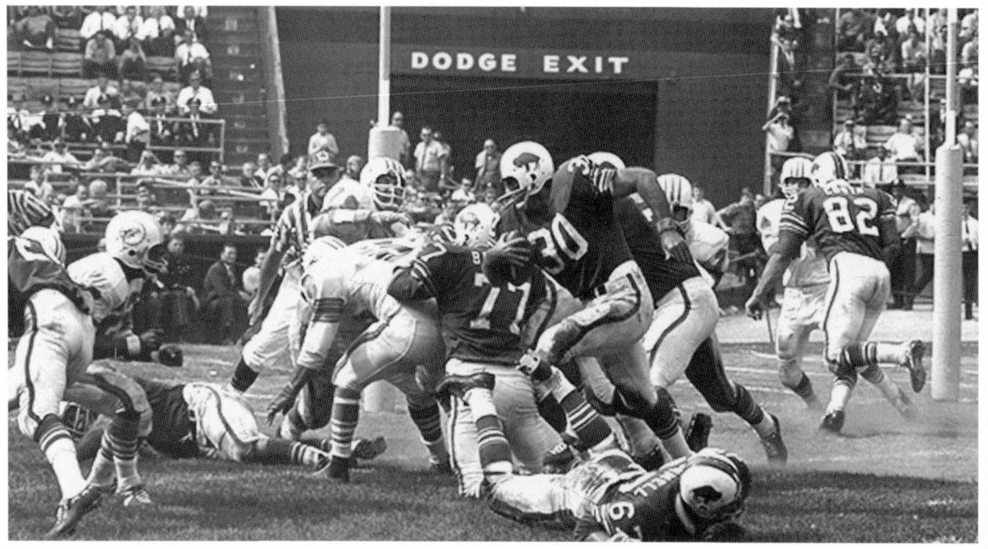

Wray Carlton #30 heads for the Dodge Street entrance at War Memorial, against the Dolphins.

Calvin Murphy was almost a regular at the half-time festivities. He was a local resident from Niagara University who twirled a baton and went on to become a star in the National Basketball Association.

The **roller coaster** was poised at the top of the hill as we added some familiar names to our roster: Paul Guidry, Mike Dennis, and Bobby Burnett. But there was trouble brewing in the coaching ranks as Lou Saban resigned his position to become the head coach at the University of Maryland. Within a few days we announced the hiring of the youngest head coach in the pros, Joe Collier, at thirty-three years of age. To make matters worse, we lost the likes of Billy Joe, Bo Roberson, Jim Davidson, and Howard Simpson to the expansion team the Miami Dolphins. Pete Gogolak became the first player in the AFL to jump leagues, joining the New York Giants. Our new kicker, Booth Lustig, had an interesting career in Buffalo. He was attacked at his home when angry fans complained about his missing a last-second field goal. Once again the Bills won the East title, with 9 wins, 4 losses, and one tie. We traveled to Kansas City and got trounced by the Chiefs 31-7. The **coaster** was headed down.

1966

Jack Kemp #15 on a road trip with his arm in a bucket of ice.

Coca-Cola
Coca-Cola

1966

Billy Shaw #66 in Bills' dressing room praying after game.

Paul Maguire #55 holds an ice bag on his head in this bench photo.

The field at War Memorial as fans go wild tearing down goal posts when Bills win East Division.

Dr. Joe Godfrey (center of photo) was the Bills' orthopedic surgeon for many years. He died at his retirement home in Maryland in 1996.

1966

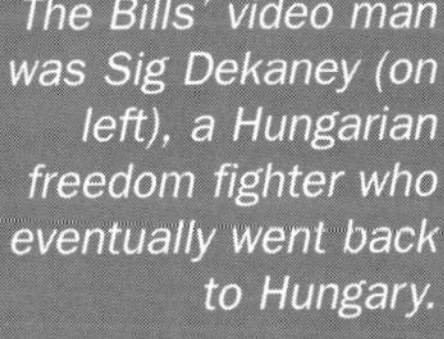

Bobby Burnett #83 and Paul Maguire #55 against Miami.

Celebration time again as we win East Division...Elbert Dubenion #44, Ed Rutkowski #40, Paul Costa #82, and Charley Ferguson #80 all celebrate after defeating Broncos 38-21.

The Bills' video man was Sig Dekaney (on left), a Hungarian freedom fighter who eventually went back to Hungary.

Bobby Burnett #21 in action as he is led by Joe O'Donnell #67; and Billy Shaw #66.

Hang onto your hats, folks! The **roller coaster** swung out of control and headed down. A new face that arrived on the Buffalo roster was Keith Lincoln from the Chargers. We traded Daryle Lamonica and Glen Bass to the Raiders for Tom Flores and Art Powell. Our first draft choice was John Pitts, and our new field goal kicker was Mike Mercer. We also suffered our first shutout loss in 142 games as we were beaten by the Patriots. Coach Lou Saban of the Broncos returned to beat the Bills 21-20. The Bills were the winners of only 4 games and lost 10. But the **coaster** had not hit the bottom yet.

The 1967 Buffalo Jills.

Hagood Clarke #45 returns a ball in a night game at War Memorial, Buffalo.

Tommy Janik #27 and George Saimes #26 look for contact lenses in the bench area.

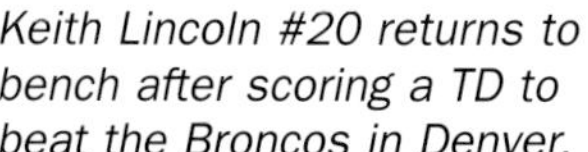

Keith Lincoln #20 returns to bench after scoring a TD to beat the Broncos in Denver.

(Left to right) Jack Kemp #15, Assistant Coach John Mazur, Tom Flores #16, and Coach Collier during a tense time in our first losing season.

Ed Rutkowski #40 makes one of his famous catches.

Mike Stratton at his locker during our skid of losses.

Jack Kemp #15 gets ready to let a bomb go....

A mud-covered Ron McDole #72 with Jim Dunaway #78 on the sidelines.

1967

Butch Byrd #42 intercepts. Behind him is Booker Edgerson #24.

Jack Kemp #15 after a very muddy 21-20 loss in Buffalo against the Denver Broncos.

The 1968 team as seen through the fish-eye lens.

The **roller coaster** was plunging so fast that we all held our breath waiting for the bottom. The first draft choice was Haven Moses, but in turn we lost Bobby Burnett to the expansion club, the Cincinnati Bengals. Bob Kalsu joined the team as our 8th draft choice and became in later years pro football's first and only casualty of the Vietnam War. We opened our first training camp at Niagara University, moving from the Blasdell NY location where we had trained for five years. Joe O'Donnell and Jack Kemp were both lost for the year with injuries early in the season. Coach Collier lasted only two games (both losses) and was replaced by Harvey Johnson. The replacement for Jack Kemp was Dan Darragh, and a new kicker was added by the name of Bruce Alford. The Bills lost 10, won 1, and tied 1. To make matters worse, Coach Johnson asked to be relieved of his coaching duties after the season. Because of this poor season we were able to obtain the rights to a player named O.J. Simpson in the 1969 draft. The **coaster** would begin another climb next year.

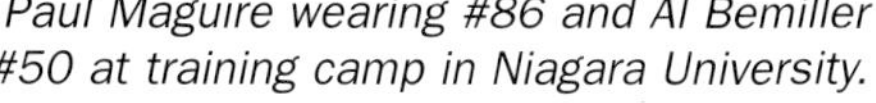
Paul Maguire wearing #86 and Al Bemiller #50 at training camp in Niagara University.

Jack Kemp #15 signs autographs for kids at Niagara University training camp.

Coach Harvey Johnson (check coat) is hired. Others, left to right: Jack Horrigan, Bob Lustig, Ralph Wilson, and Pat McGroeder give him a welcome from the front office.

Daryle Lamonica #3, still with the Raiders, led his team to a 48-6 victory and sealed the fate of Coach Joe Collier.

Harvey Johnson, new head coach...alone with his thoughts.

Ron McDole #72 blocks a field goal attempt by the Patriots.

1968

Paul Guidry #59 makes a great play against Matt Snell of the Jets. Our only win of the year, 37-35.

Harvey Johnson gets the handshake of a winner from Weeb Ewbank, Jets coach. It will be Johnson's only victory as a head coach in 1968.

Tom Day #89 put pressure on the Miami QB Bob Griese.

Ed Rutkowski #40 comes out of the game as trainer Ed Abramoski (on right) walks with him.

This is what happened to Rookies in the old days. That's Paul Costa with the clippers as Paul Maguire holds the ears of Haven Moses.

Coach John Rauch and Jack Kemp on the sidelines.

Marty Schottenheimer #57, who went on to become a head coach, and Coach John Rauch in the bench area.

Gary McDermott #32 would not relinquish his number to O.J. Simpson , who was given #36.

Butch Byrd #42 intercepts a pass and returns it for a TD vs. Broncos in War Memorial Stadium.

The year started with a flourish as O.J. Simpson was drafted #1 by Buffalo, who had just completed the worst record in professional football for 1968. Our head coach Harvey Johnson was replaced by John Rauch of the Oakland Raiders who was given an unprecedented four-year contract. Our old coach Joe Collier went to the Broncos with Lou Saban. Bob Kalsu #61 was inducted into the U.S. Army and was lost for the season. With the roller coaster on the way up from the bottom, we signed O.J. Simpson, who was met at the airport by over 2,000 fans, including Mayor Frank Sedita. A few of the new players in camp that year were Marlin Brisco, Bill "Earthquake" Enyart, and James Harris, a QB from Grambling. We lost, due to retirement or waivers, the likes of Haygood Clarke, Bill Flint, and Tom Sestak, Tom Day, Ed Rutkowski, and Marty Schottenheimer. The Bills won a game on September 28 and it was their first win in almost one year. In November the Bills lost their 13th straight road game and things were looking a bit dismal. Jack Kemp played his last game in 1969 and finished his career with 77 touchdown passes. We won a few more times, with a grand total of 4 wins and 12 losses, so it looked like the coaster had finally bottomed out and was climbing again.

1969

O.J. arrives in Buffalo for first time, greeted by Mayor Frank Sedita and Miss Buffalo. Behind O.J. is Jack Horrigan, the Public Relations Director of the Bills.

O.J. being drafted by Bills staff (standing left to right): Coach John Rauch, Ralph Wilson, and Harvey Johnson.

O.J. makes his debut (wearing #36) at Los Angeles Rams. We were beaten 50-20, with O.J. gaining 20 yards.

The New York State Erie County Legislators as they tour the Astrodome in Houston, Texas, looking for ideas for a new stadium.

This was against the Broncos as O.J. had his first 100-yard rushing day. Here he makes for daylight as seen from the press box on September 28, 1969.

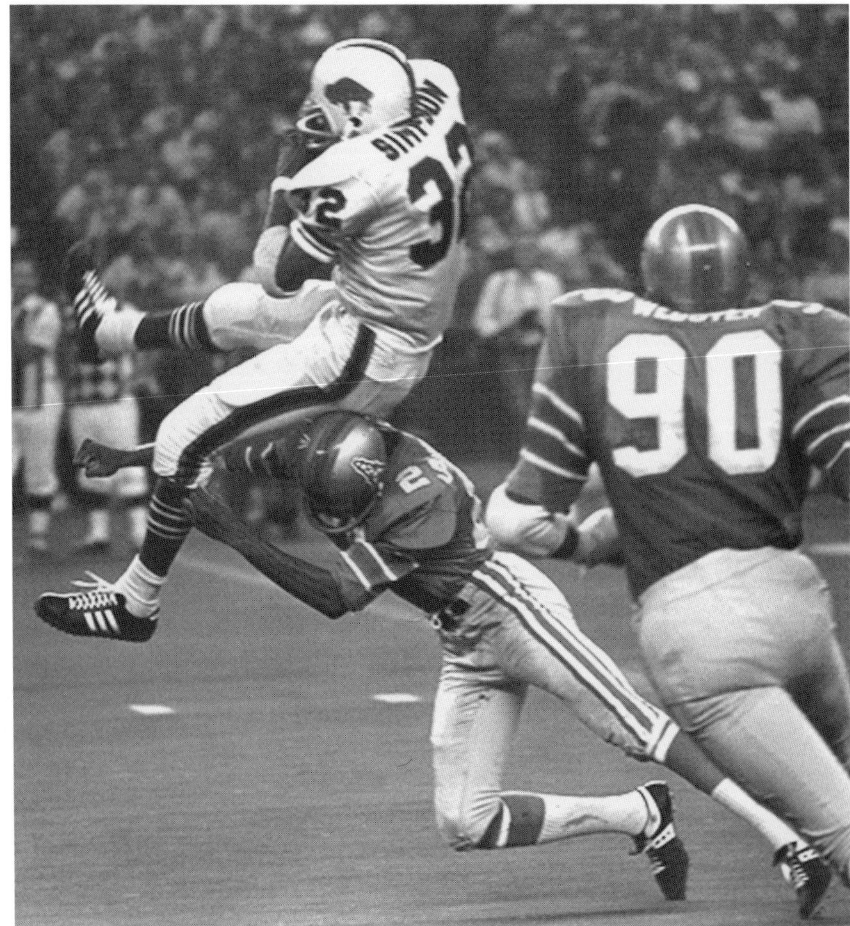

O.J. in action vs. Oilers.

1969

Bill "Earthquake" Enyart gets outfitted at Bills training camp by Tony Marchitte and Ron Krauza.

Thc Bills QBs Jack Kemp #15, Tom Flores #16, and Kay Stephenson #18 on Bills sidelines.

The **roller coaster** took a slight dip from our 4 wins in 1969 and continued to plummet as we managed 3 wins with 10 losses and 1 tie. A familiar name on the roster, Stu Barber #77, retired but in later years became the general manager of the Bills. Others who retired this year were Jack Kemp and Billy Shaw. Kemp made it known he would try for Congress in the 39th District of New York State. On July 21 it was announced that Bob Kalsu, on leave from the Bills, was killed in action in Vietnam, becoming the only professional player in the league to be killed in the war. A player's strike loomed in the early part of the year but was averted prior to the opening game. Another familiar name that was traded was Booker Edgerson (he also came back to make Buffalo his home town), and Coach Rauch then cut Al Bemiller, George Saimes, and Harry Jacobs. In October the Miami Dolphins, with Coach Shula making his debut in Buffalo, beat the Bills 33-14. Later in the year we broke our 14-game losing streak for road games by beating the Jets. We drafted Al Cowlings from U.S.C. as our first draft choice, then picked Dennis Shaw, a quarterback from San Diego, as #2. Wayne Patrick and Mike Stratton were lost for the rest of the season with injuries, and the **coaster** continued downward.

Edgar Chandler #52 with the ball as he heads for the end zone.

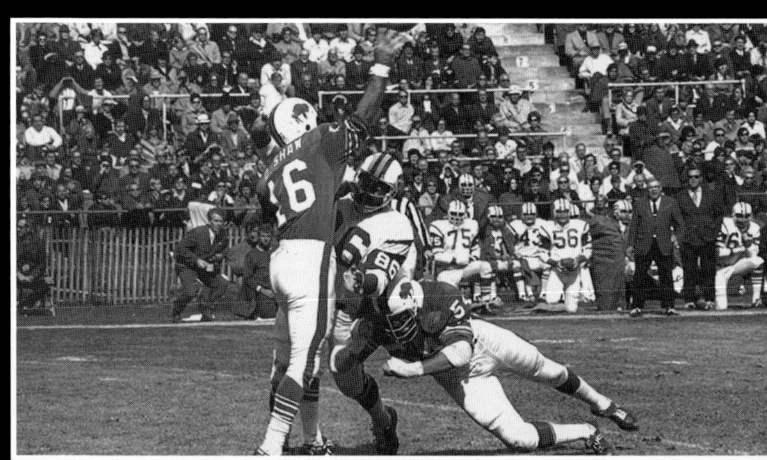

Dennis Shaw #16, our new rookie QB, in action.

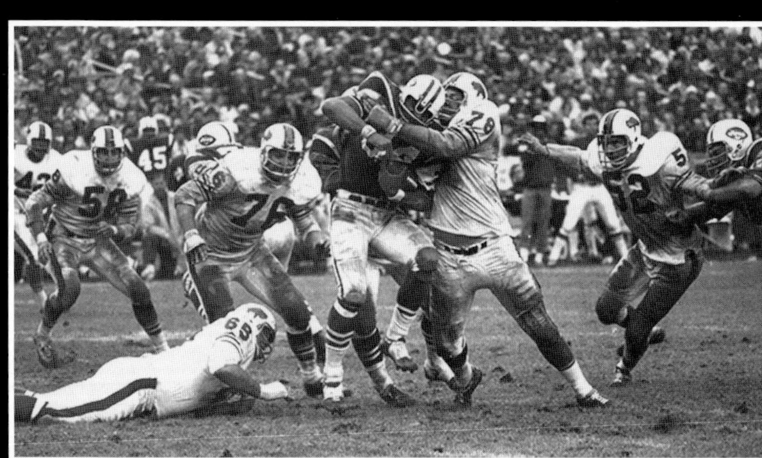

Jim Dunaway #78 stops a Jets player as Mike McBath #76 and Edgar Chandler #52 come on strong.

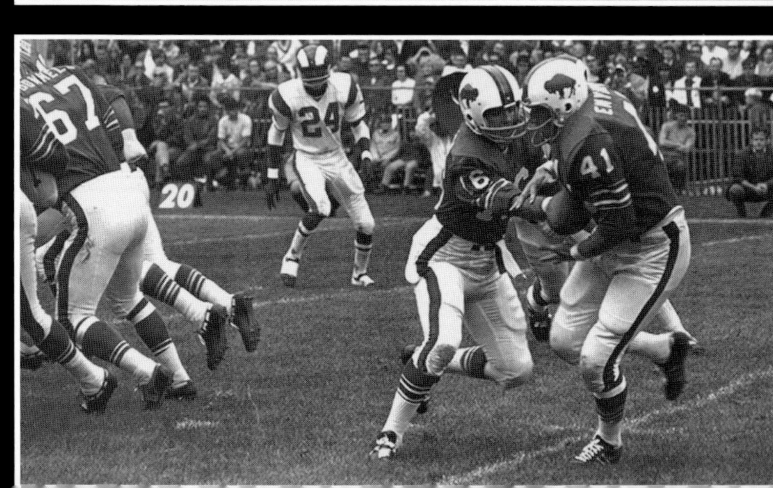

Dennis Shaw #16 hands off to Bill "Earthquake" Enyart as we play the Rams.

James Harris #12, one of our QBs, in action against the Patriots. At presstime, James is the Assistant General Manager of the New York Jets.

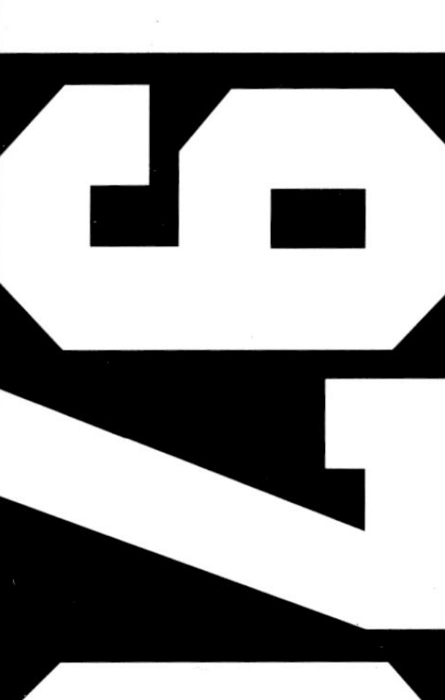

O.J. Simpson #32 soars over the Eagles, rushing for 77 yards.

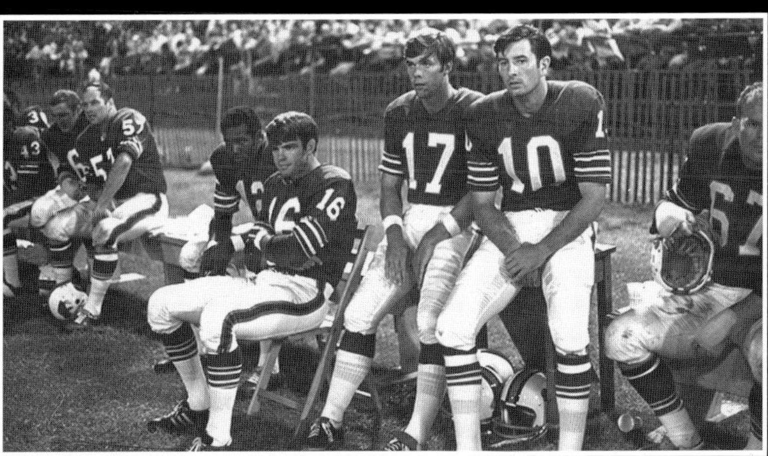

A couple of quarterbacks on the sidelines...Left to right: Dennis Shaw #16 and Dan Darragh #10.

Al Cowlings #82 on the bench.

Left to right: Ron McDole #72 and Jim Dunaway #78 visit with their newly retired teammate Tom Sestak.

Spectators express their wishes for a dome.

The tarp being rolled up on one of the many cold and snowy days in War Memorial Stadium in downtown Buffalo.

The team of the '60s is honored. Here Elbert Dubenion presents a jersey to Mr. Wilson with his name on it. Seated is the late Paul Neville, the managing editor of the Buffalo News. *The '60s team was on the field the next day for festivities and a group photo.*

Wayne Patrick #30 takes a break from the action.

Coach Rauch bids goodbye to Billy Shaw on his retirement as Mrs. Shaw listens.

Mike Stratton #58 makes a lunge for Patriots QB.

The Bills bench. The wood platform in front of players was to keep mud out of their cleats.

Muddy War Memorial Stadium.

Marlin Brisco #86 on his way to a TD on a pass from Dennis Shaw, vs. Dallas on Sept. 19.

1971

We thought we were at the bottom of the **roller coaster ride** in 1970, but this year proved to be even worse as we ended up with a **one-win season** with 13 losses. We started off by drafting J.D. Hill #1, then Jan White, Bruce Jarvis, Jim Braxton, Donnie Green, and Bobby Chandler. We also traded Bill Enyart to Oakland for Alvin Wyatt and Ron McDole to Washington where he became an instant starter for the Redskins. Tom Day came back to the Bills as their defensive line coach and became the first black assistant coach in the Bills organization. Paul Maguire made his retirement official and started his broadcasting career. Head Coach John Rauch resigned in preseason training camp. Harvey Johnson once again took control of the team as head coach, and this all happened prior to the start of the season. We won our first game on November 28, Harvey Johnson's second career win as head coach. In the meantime we lost two games in succession by shutouts. On December 19 our worst season came to an end and the **roller coaster** hit rock bottom again. On December 23 the Bills gave a Christmas present to Lou Saban by rehiring him to guide the Bills in the future, replacing Harvey Johnson. With a record of 1 and 13 the fans were looking for drastic improvements.

Dennis Shaw #16 and Haven Moses #25 sign autographs on autograph day.

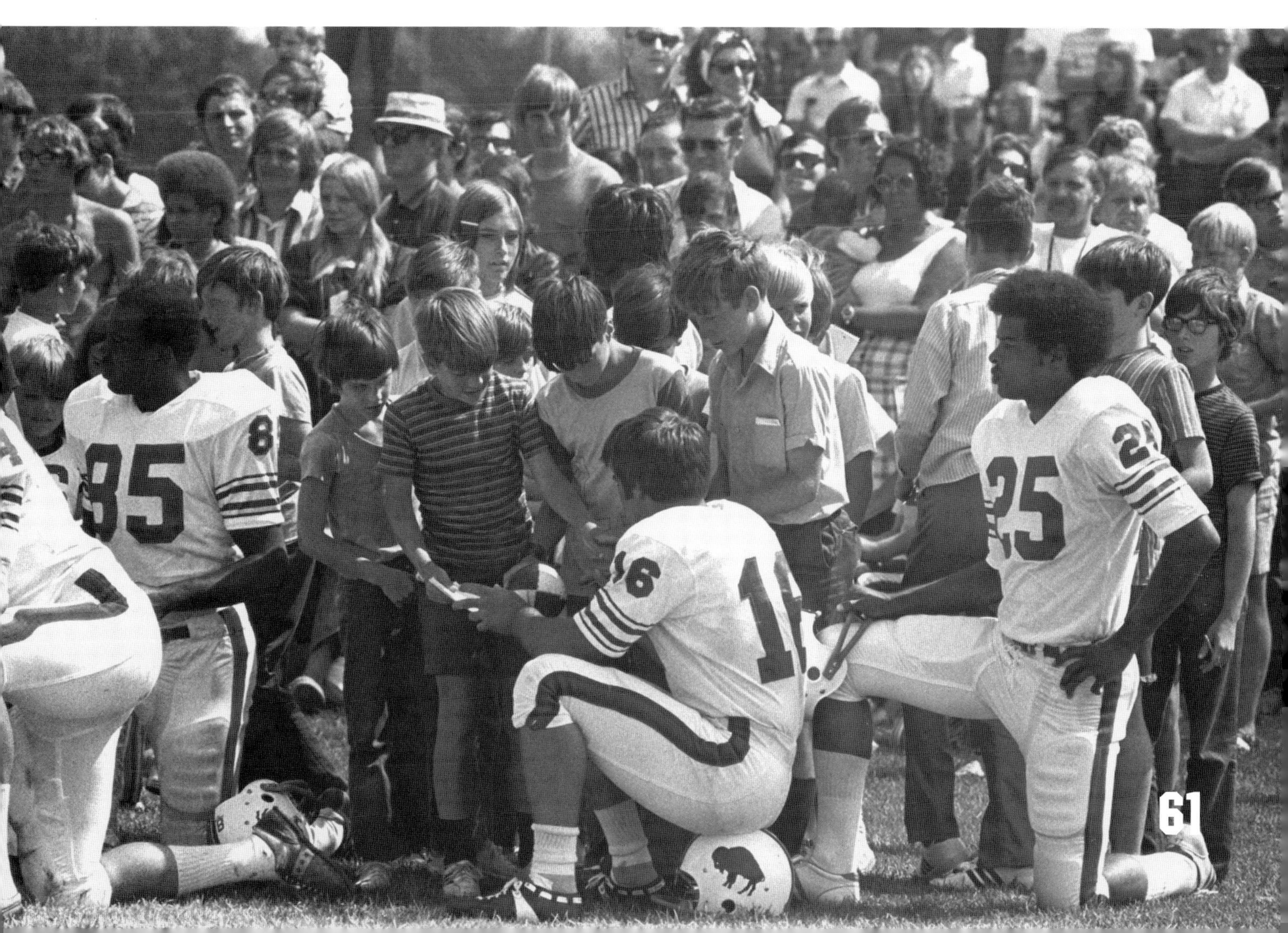

J.D. Hill #40, our first draft choice.

Wayne Patrick #30 in the dressing room after another loss.

New coach Harvey Johnson on far left with his coaching staff.

Ron Krauza, assistant equipment manager, Tony Marchitte, equipment manager and Ed Abramoski, trainer, pose for press photo.

Lou Saban being named new head coach by Harvey Johnson.

The ref gets in the way of this play and gets some rough treatment from Paul Guidry #59.

Bobby Chandler #81 makes a great try for this pass against the Eagles.

Haven Moses #25 in action against the Packers.

Edgar Chandler #52 and Al Cowlings #82 during a practice.

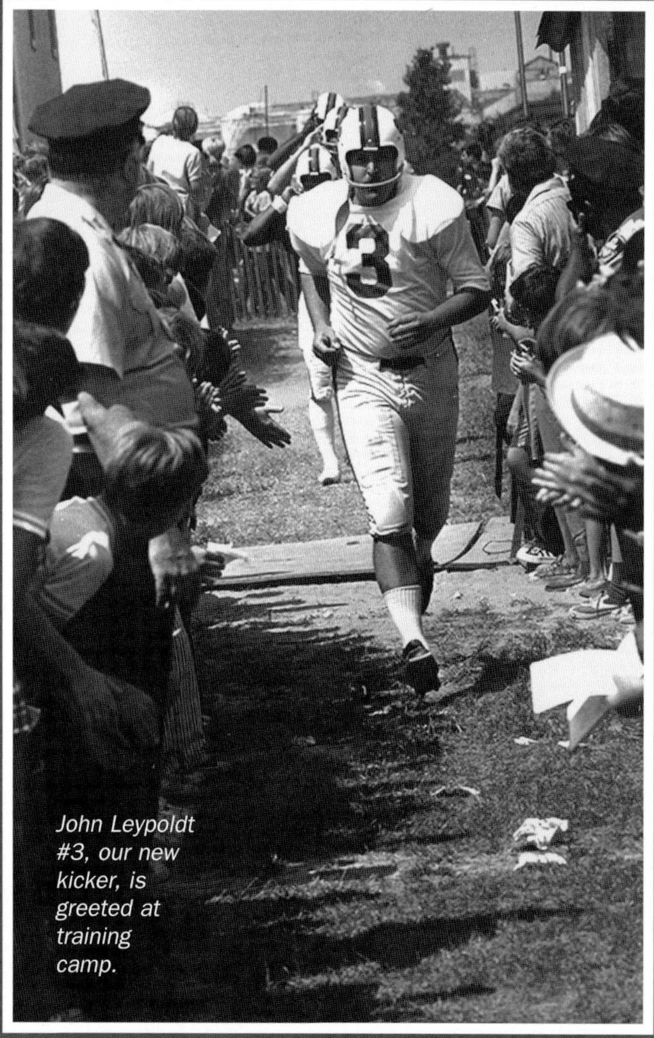

John Leypoldt #3, our new kicker, is greeted at training camp.

Coach Lou Saban took over the head coaching job for the second time in six years and started by replacing all assistant coaches. We made Walt Patulski our #1 draft choice and picked Reggie McKenzie as #2. The **roller coaster** had no where to go but up. Ground-breaking ceremonies were held in Orchard Park to start construction of a new 80,000 seat stadium that was to be called Rich Stadium. Receiver Malin Briscoe and Jim Dunaway were traded to Miami, and Jack Kemp was elected to Congress. John Leypoldt was our new kicker and we were ready to go. Quarterback James Harris was waived and we signed Mike Taliaferro in his place. Even though we beat San Francisco 27-20, we were shutout again by the Colts for the third straight time. By October 8 we had already increased our win percentage by 100% over 1971 with our second win of the year. Another name player was traded in October, Haven Moses for Dwight Harrison. By mid-November we finally ended a 5-game losing streak and a 13-game road losing streak. O.J. Simpson topped the 1,000-yard rushing mark for the first time, but we still lost to Cleveland. On December 10 we played our last game in War Memorial Stadium and tied the Lions. Our final game was in Washington, where O.J. won the rushing title with 1,251 yards on 292 carries. Slowly the **coaster** was gaining speed as we finished the season with 4 wins, 9 losses, and 1 tie.

One of the last games to be played in the Old Rock Pile...War Memorial Stadium.

1972

Frustrations....with a 10 game losing season.

Mike Stratton #58 shows the form of going after Miami QB Earl Morrall making his first start.

A spectacular play as J.D. Hill #40 is upended in the shutout loss to the Colts.

O.J. Simpson #32 in War Memorial Stadium vs. the Cleveland Browns.

1972

The start of new stadium as (left to right) Coach Lou Saban, Ralph Wilson, Bob Lustig, and Jack Horrigan all turn a spadeful of dirt to start construction.

A happy moment at practice as Tony Marchitte, the equipment manager, dresses as a player for Coach Saban and asks to have a tryout for the Bills.

Coach Lou Saban on the sidelines...letting his voice be heard.

The end of an era as the goal posts come down at War Memorial Stadium after our last game vs. Lions.

A tryout for ushers for the new Stadium to be opened soon in Orchard Park.

Dwight Harrison #21 wins the game for the Bills after he returns an interception for the final score against the Colts in Maryland 24-17.

Johnny Unitas of the Chargers has his hands full with a pass rush from the Bills.

We started out the year by pulling straws to see where we would pick in the draft. We selected Paul Seymour from Michigan as our #1 draft choice, then selected Joe DeLamielleure from Michigan State. The **roller coaster** was beginning to move upward as we finally finished with a decent season, winning 9 and losing 5. Other players added to the Bills roster that year were Jeff Yeates, Bob Kampa, John Skorpan, Wallace Francis, and Merv Krakau. We lost a good friend when Jack Horrigan, the public relations director, died of cancer at age 47. L. Budd Thalman was hired to handle the PR for the Bills. We started playing in our new home, Rich Stadium, in Orchard Park, New York. On the first play of the game, Herb Mul-Key of the Washington Redskins returned the kick-off 102 yards for a touchdown. Also on the team was our third draft choice, Joe Ferguson, a quarterback whose name would become synonymous with O.J. Simpson. Two other trades that took place prior to the start of the season were Mike Kadish for Irv Goode and Mike Stratton for a future draft choice. Our opener brought a record for O.J. when he rushed for 250 yards in defeating New England 31-13. In October we played our first Monday Night Football Game and beat Kansas City, with O.J. reaching the 1,000-yard mark in just 7 games. In November the entire team was given a scare when our plane had hydraulic trouble, and we landed in Cleveland with our heads firmly between our knees. The name "The Electric Company" was given to the offensive line as they "turned on the Juice" (O.J. Simpson). On Dec 16 history was made in New York's Shea Stadium as O.J. surpassed the old record of Jim Brown and went 2,003 yards for the year, but we did not make the playoffs. Up we go on the **coaster** as we look forward to 1974.

1973

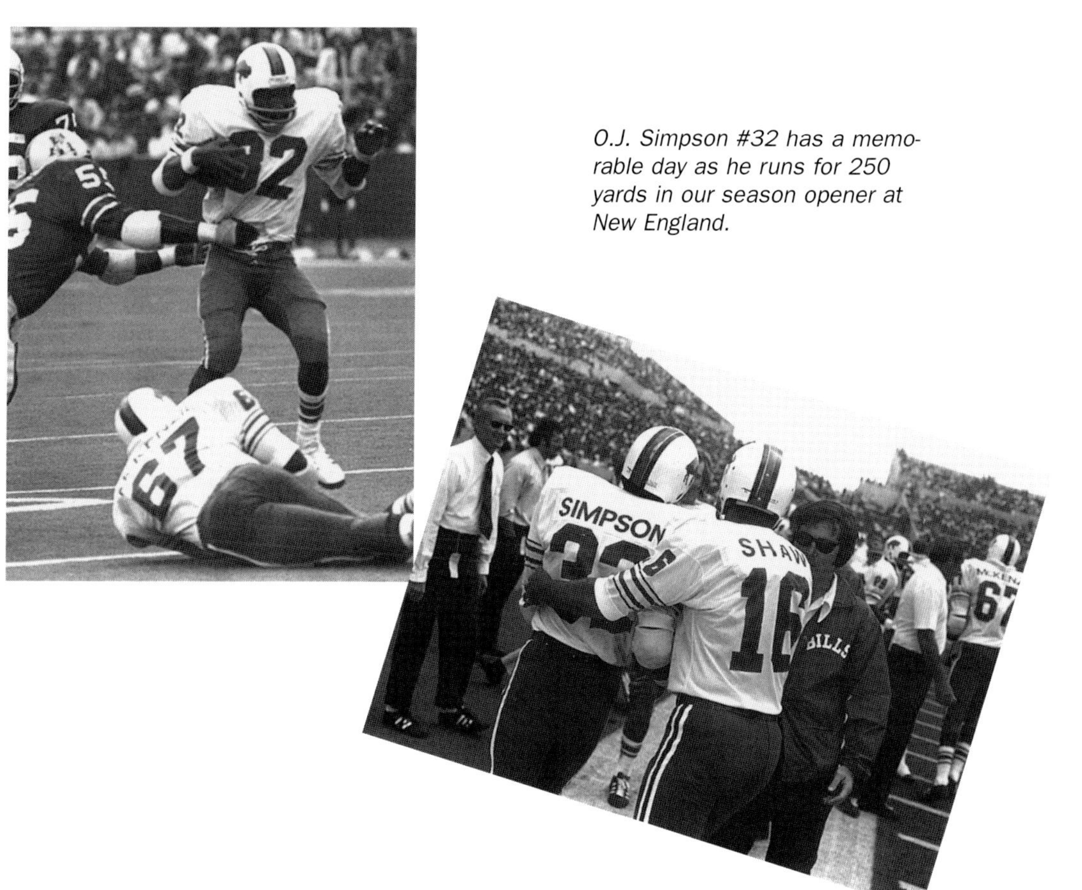

O.J. Simpson #32 has a memorable day as he runs for 250 yards in our season opener at New England.

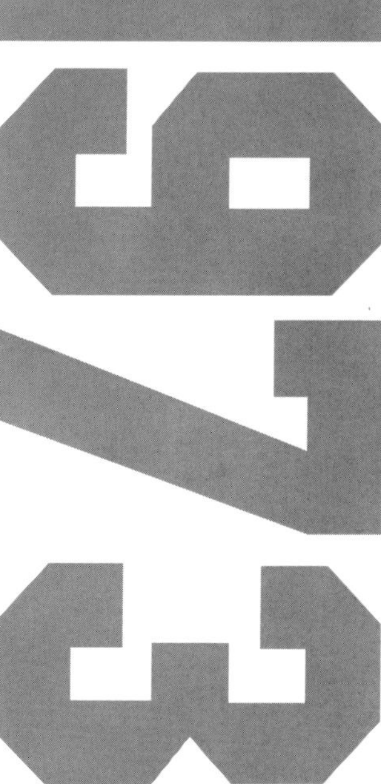

Opening festivities at the new stadium in Orchard Park.

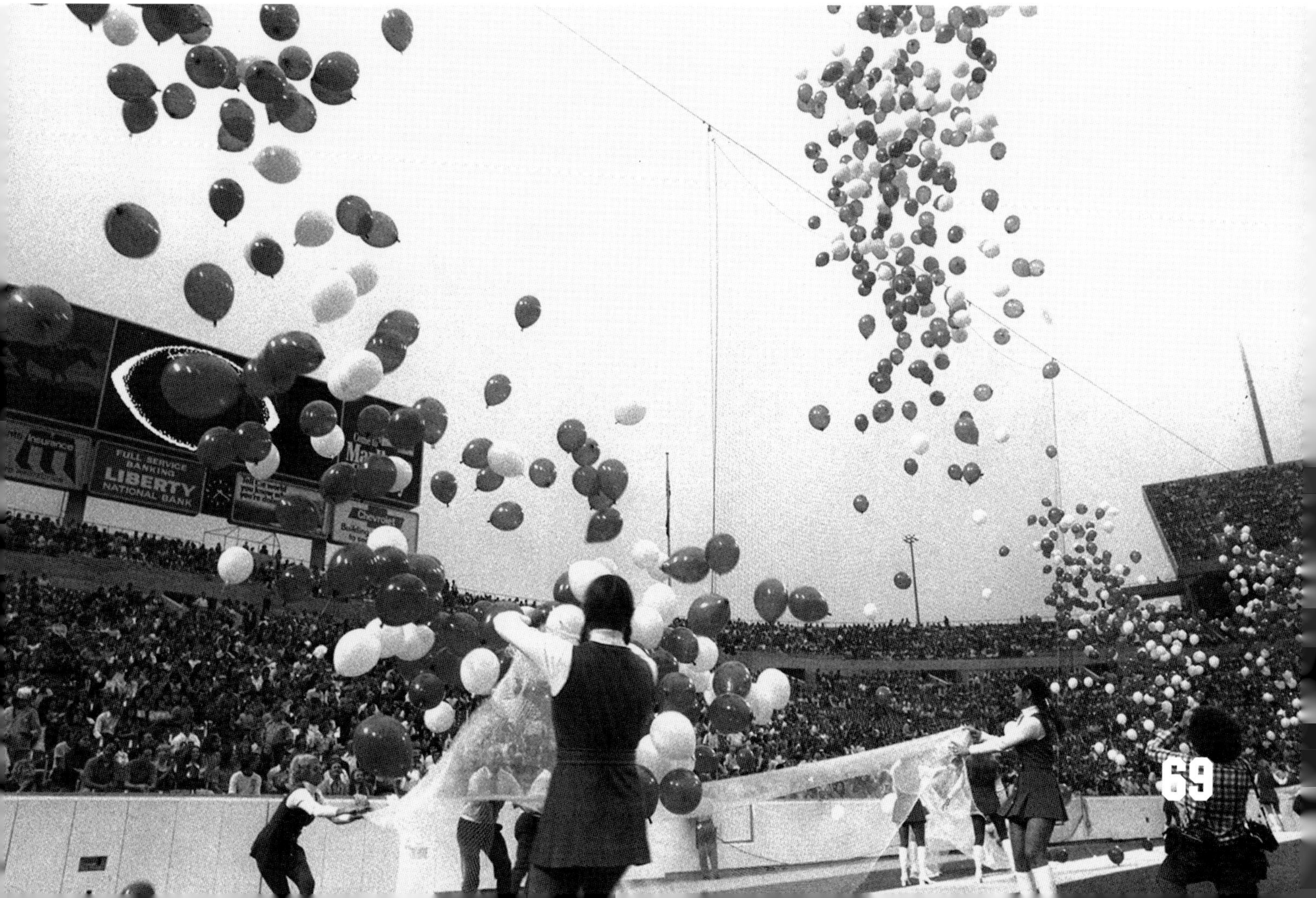

2,003 YARDS FOR O.J. SIMPSON #32! *Versus the Jets in New York, Dec. 16. This was the actual play where he went over the 2,000-yard mark.*

O.J. is carried off the playing field by his teammates after achieving the 2,003-yard record.

O.J. removes his clothes, which were all saved for the Pro Football Hall of Fame, where they are now on display.

O.J. in the dressing room as he speaks to Rick Azar of WKBW TV and Robert L. Smith, the Bills photographer.

L. Budd Thalman, the public relations director, on the sidelines with Ralph Wilson on a low day for the Bills as we were defeated by the Saints 13-0 in New Orleans.

This is the photo of O.J. achieving his 2,003 yards that was on display in Orchard Park, NY for years.

1973

Bobby Chandler #81 makes a spectacular catch at Atlanta. He became quite famous for acrobatic pass receptions. Chandler died of cancer in 1995.

Coach Lou Saban waits to talk to the team after a loss on the road.

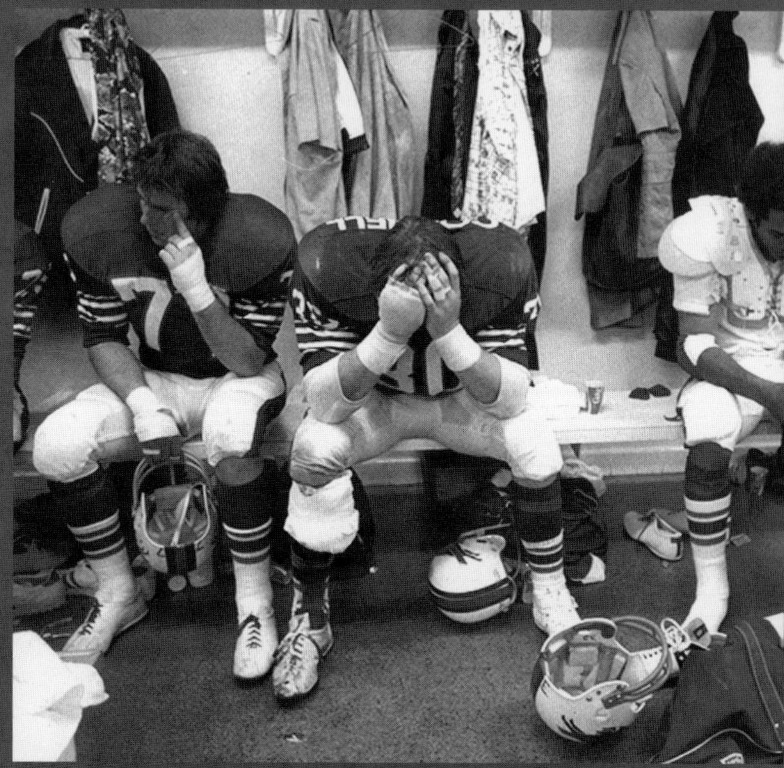

The Bills' dressing room after a frustrating loss.

Ahmad Rashad #27 gets emotional on the sidelines as Pittsburgh defeats the Bills in playoffs 32-14.

Our **roller coaster ride** leveled off this year and stayed at 9 wins and 5 losses, but we did manage to get into the playoffs against the Pittsburgh Steelers. Early in the year we traded Dennis Shaw for Ahmad Rashad and selected Reuben Gant from Oklahoma State as our #1; we then selected Doug Allen second and Gary Marangi third. On June 30 the players went on strike, sending everyone into a tailspin as the teams struggled to fill all spots on their rosters with rookies and free agents. The "counterfeit" Bills played their first game in Canton, Ohio, and lost to St. Louis 21-13. In mid-August the players' strike was crumbling, with veterans regularly crossing the lines, and soon the strike was considered over with all veterans in camp. In September the Bills played their second Monday Night Football Game and defeated the Oakland Raiders in a thriller 21-20. This was the year another odd phenomenon occurred when Buffalo played an entire game with no passes being completed but still defeated the Jets 16-12 on a very windy day. In the beginning of November the Bills defeated the Patriots in Massachusetts for first place in the AFC East and were met at the airport by a very large crowd of fans. The Miami Dolphins defeated the Bills for the 10th time in a row, but later the Bills did manage to gain a spot in the AFC playoffs. We were defeated by the Pittsburgh Steelers, but it was a bit of consolation when they eventually won the Super Bowl.

O.J. Simpson and kids. He always signed autographs and posed for photos with everyone who showed up at practice.

Joe Namath #12 of Jets gets rough treatment in what was rumored to be Joe's last game in Shea Stadium. New York won 20-10.

Mike Montler #53 covered with mud in 16-6 win over the Chicago Bears.

The kick that missed by George Blanda in the final seconds of the Monday Night Football Game. The Bills won with two TDs by Ahmad Rashad.

1974

Coach Lou Saban shows his emotions after a game when he kisses Tony Greene #43 as they leave the field in Rich Stadium. We defeated the Patriots 30-28.

Offensive Line Coach Jim Ringo was given a game ball after we defeated the Green Bay Packers. He was once a Packers player.

A difference of opinions...The ref and Joe Ferguson #12...Guess who won?

Two #12s leave the field of battle...On left is Joe Ferguson with Joe Namath.

Joe DeLamielleure #68 in action, otherwise known as "Joe D".

This is the wire walker who made network TV when he climbed out on the guide wires holding the net during a Monday Night Football Game. He was arrested as soon as he was coaxed down.

John Holland #80 with the game ball he was awarded by teammates for his play against the Colts when he made a 62-yard reception, setting up the winning TD.

We started out the year by selecting Tom Ruud from Nebraska as our first draft choice and then his teammate, Bob Nelson #2, followed by Roland Hooks from North Carolina. This was the year that the **roller coaster** stayed pretty level as we won 8 and lost 6 with no playoff game. Coach Saban made the 50th trade of his tenure with the Bills by trading Larry Watkins to the Giants for a draft choice. Former Bills tackle Stew Barber rejoined the organization as a talent scout. This was also the year that the Rolling Stones played in Rich Stadium to over 70,000 fans. Steve Freeman arrived from New England, and Ruud and Nelson signed their first pro contracts in late August and early September. The season started off well with the Bills beating the Jets and O.J. having a banner game with 173 rushing yards. We beat the defending Super Bowl Champions, the Pittsburgh Steelers, for our second win in as many starts, and again O.J. had a fantastic day with 227 yards rushing. We went on to win four in a row before being stopped by the Giants 17-14 in a Monday night game. This was also the game where a fan hung on the cable used to support the net behind the goal posts, and we received some very unfavorable TV coverage. The World Football League officially folded in October, and the NFL was inundated with players looking for jobs. In late October the Miami Dolphins beat the Bills for their 11th straight victory with a 4th quarter rally. The two expansion clubs, Seattle and Tampa Bay, were getting ready to invade the talent that was unprotected in the NFL. Rumors were also flying that Ralph Wilson and Coach Lou Saban were at odds about trades that Saban wished to make. On December 7 the Miami Dolphins beat the Bills for the 12th consecutive time and eliminated the Bills from the playoffs. Close to Christmas on a snowy day in Orchard Park, O.J. Simpson set another NFL record for touchdowns in a year (23); but that was clouded by the snowball barrage that rained down on the Vikings, causing one of their players to possibly miss a playoff game. The Super Bowl was played with the Steelers winning their second in a row, but this time Dallas was the loser.

Steve Freeman #22 joined the Bills in 1975 and played for 12 years.

O.J. Simpson and Joe Namath walk off the field in N.Y. after Bills beat the Jets 24-23. O.J. scored once, caught 2 passes for 66 yards, and rushed 21 times for 94 yards.

UPPER LEFT: Dr. Joe Godfrey on the sidelines...Always watching the play and even getting thrown out of a game for letting his opinion be known to the referees.
LEFT: Paul Seymour #87 makes a great catch against the Bengals to show why he was drafted #l.
TOP: Coach Saban and Joe Ferguson #12 on the sidelines as #17 Gary Marangi listens.

O.J. Simpson poses for press photos by leaping over a photographer so he can get "The Right Angle.

Patriots QB Steve Grogan #14 gets sacked 8 times in this 34-14 loss to the Bills in New England.

O.J. Simpson #32 swarmed under by defenders from the Colts. He still managed to gain 159 yards rushing and we won the game 38-31

THE OFFENSE as they pose for a group photo during practice.

Nelson and Ruud...First and Second round draft choices...only played for three seasons (1975-77).

As seen in this photo, the Bills of 1976 did not always play in front of a full house.

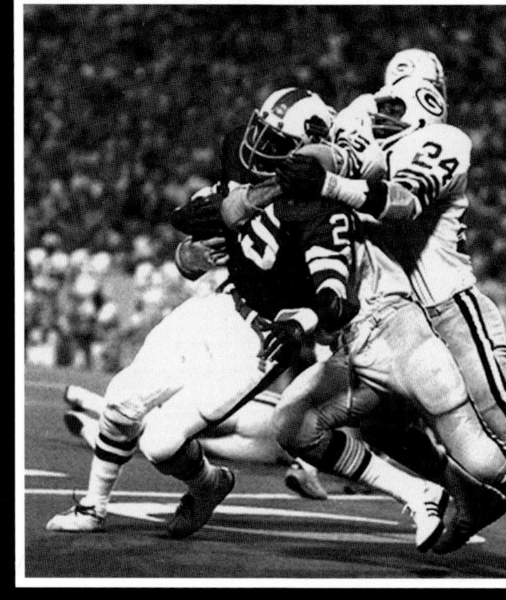

Roland Hooks # 25 as he is brought down by two Packers.

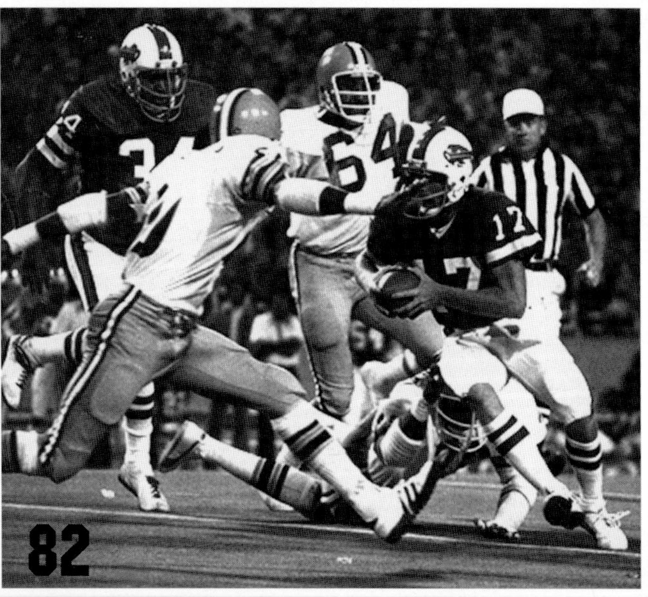

QB Gary Marangi #17 in a game against the Cleveland Browns.

The season started out on shaky ground with some of our assistant coaches leaving to take other jobs in the league and O.J. Simpson expressing his displeasure at being paid less than Joe Namath. Walt Patulski was traded away for a second-round draft choice, but we added the names of Mario Clark as our first choice, then Ken Jones, Joe Devlin, Ben Williams, Dan Jilik, and Keith Moody. With O.J. Simpson threatening to leave Buffalo and play with a West Coast team, the **roller coaster** took a dip downward as we won 2 and lost 12. The most devastating news of the year was the resignation of Coach Saban for the second time. He was replaced in mid-season by Jim Ringo. We signed O.J. Simpson to a multi-year contract and were confident that he would play his remaining years in Buffalo, since he had become the highest paid player in professional football at $2.5 million for three years. The Bills lost 9 games in a row after Coach Ringo took over the coaching helm, but a bright spot was the Thanksgiving Day game when O.J. rushed for 273 yards in a loss to Detroit 27-14. Our dismal year ended with our 14th straight loss to the Miami Dolphins, and it seemed like the **coaster** would drop even farther before starting upward.

1976

Jeff Kinney # 36, who replaced Braxton, breaks through the line of Tampa Bay.

Paul Seymour #87 and Jim Braxton #34 on the sidelines.

O.J. gets his due reward from his peers as he rushed for 273 yards at Detroit on November 25, 1976.

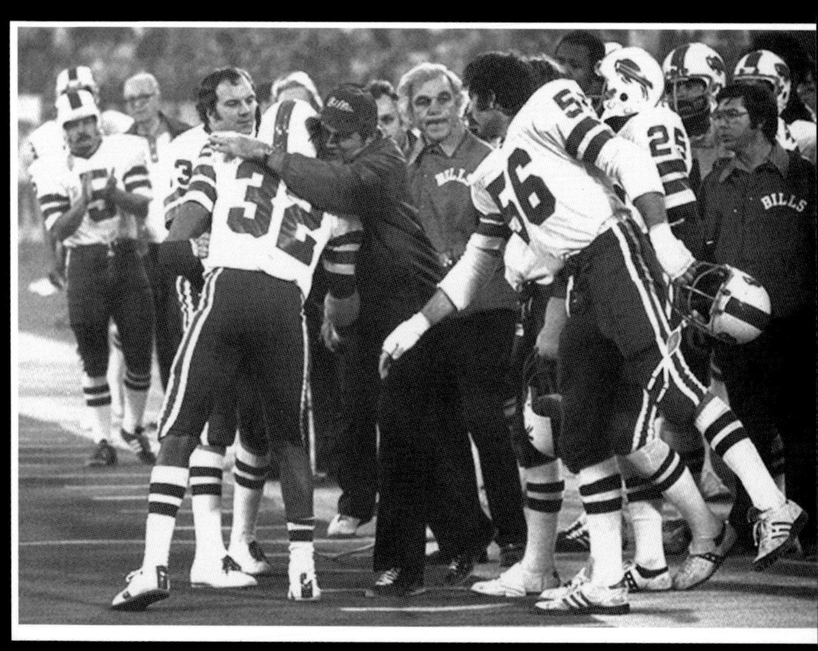

O.J. Simpson and Howard Cossell doing a taping prior to Monday night football game on ABC-TV.

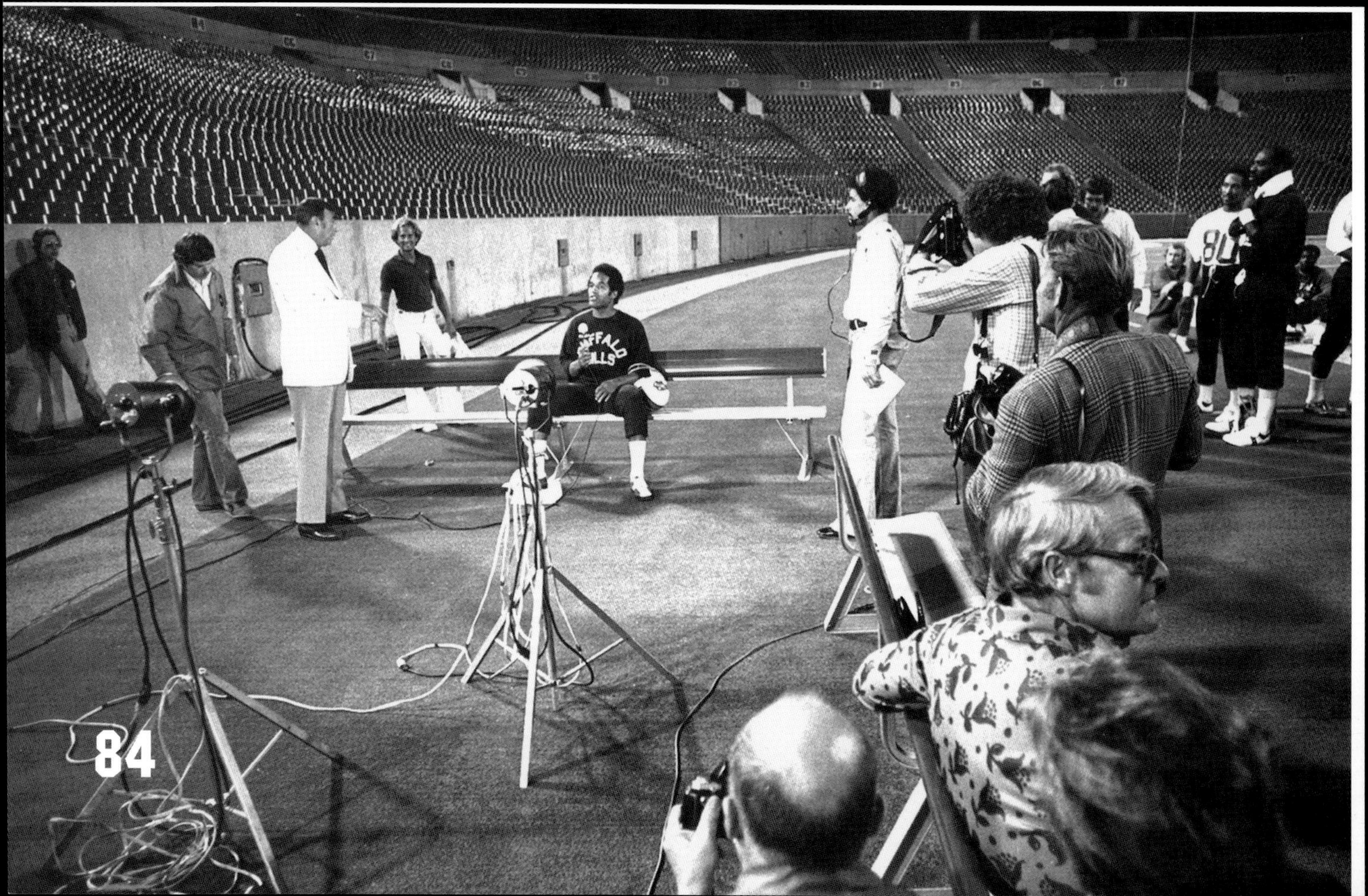

1976

Historic moment in Bills' history as O.J. and Ralph Wilson agree to terms.

The injury to Joe Ferguson that put him out for the year...against Patriots.

Coach Jim Ringo stresses a point with QB Gary Marangi #17 as the injured Joe Ferguson #12 (in rear) listens.

1976

Mike Holmes #86 of Bills, covered with mud, vs. the Jets in Shea Stadium.

A Buffalo Mascot that did not last long on the Bills' sidelines.

Jim Ringo, new head coach, shows the strains of 9 losses in a row.

Photographers on the sidelines: (top to bottom) yours truly, Bob Smith; Ron Moscati; and Jim Selover, all covering a Bills game.

Jim Kelly #12 of the Bills being sacked by the nemesis of our team Brian Cox #51 of Miami (now of the Chicago Bears.)

1990

SUPER BOWL XXV

NY GIANTS 20/BILLS 19
Tampa Stadium, Florida

Closest game in Super Bowl history as Buffalo loses in last four seconds.

THE KICK

Our First Super Bowl came to this final kick as Scott Norwood #11 misses a 47 yard field goal with 4 seconds remaining in game. We lost to the Giants 20-19.

THO
11

1991

SUPER BOWL XXVI

WASHINGTON REDSKINS 37/BILLS 24 Metrodome in Minneapolis, MN.

Kelly throws for record 58 passes, Thurman Thomas loses his helmet, and we lose our second consecutive Super Bowl.

RIGHT: A rally in downtown Buffalo to show support for the Bills was held the day after Super Bowl.

BELOW: James Lofton #80 reaches in vain for the ball as the win slips away.

1992

SUPER BOWL XXVII

DALLAS COWBOYS 52/BILLS 17

Our third consecutive Super Bowl loss (another Super Bowl record...)

MAIN PHOTO: Thurman Thomas #34 is shown getting a few of his 19 yards for the day.

INSET: Jim Kelly #12 tried his best to rally the troops.

34
80
83
88

BELOW: A happy group of Bills players as they get ready to head for their fourth Super Bowl in a row.

RIGHT: A popular group of fans that are at all Bills home games..The Bishop and his Nuns.

Bruce Smith #78 puts the pressure on Jeff Hostetler the QB during a playoff game against the Raiders in Buffalo. We won 29-23.

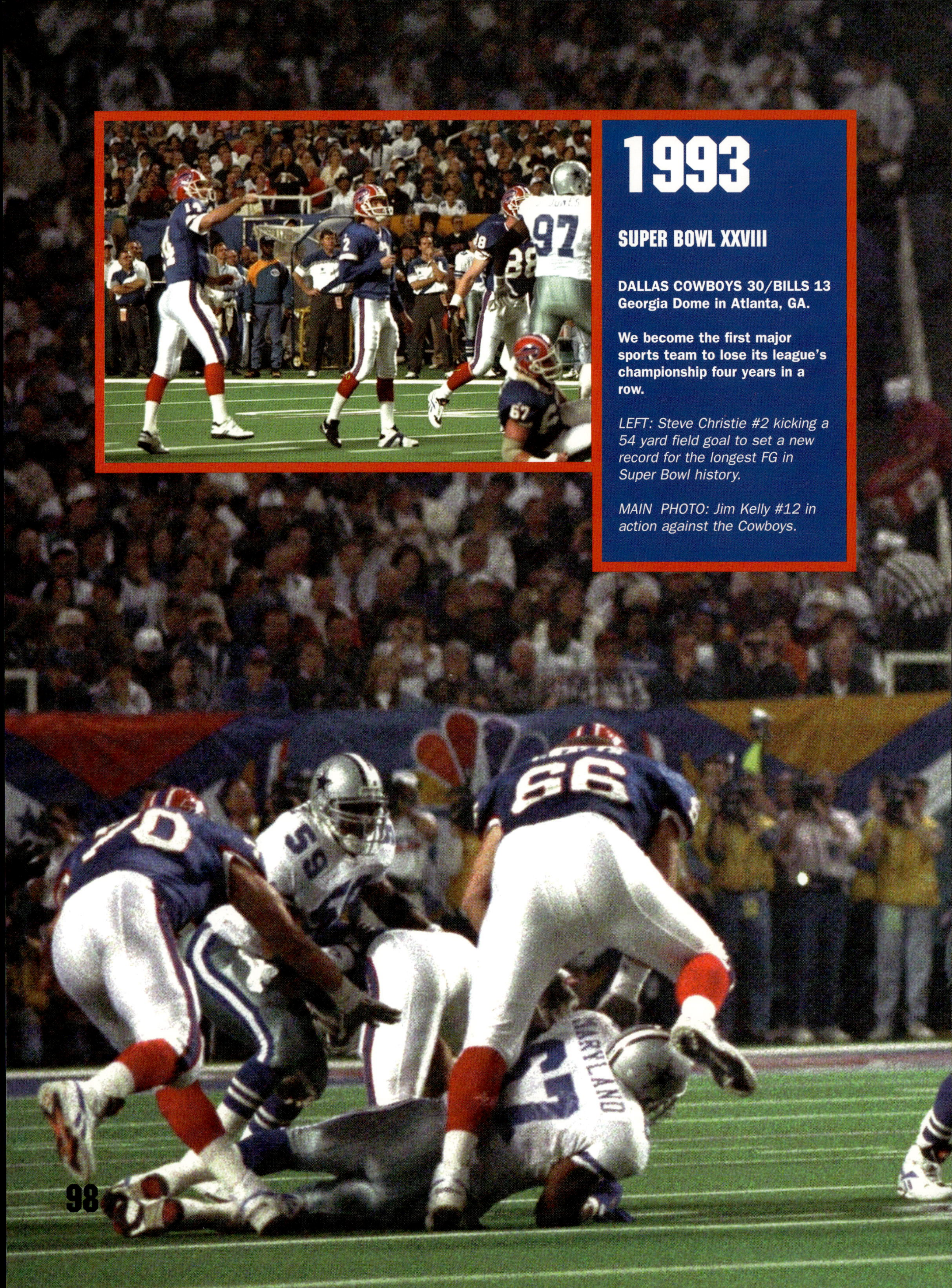

1993

SUPER BOWL XXVIII

DALLAS COWBOYS 30/BILLS 13
Georgia Dome in Atlanta, GA.

We become the first major sports team to lose its league's championship four years in a row.

LEFT: Steve Christie #2 kicking a 54 yard field goal to set a new record for the longest FG in Super Bowl history.

MAIN PHOTO: Jim Kelly #12 in action against the Cowboys.

12
23

Ed Abramoski the trainer of The Bills from 1960-1995 (semi-retired) watches his team defeat the Falcons.

Aerial photo of Rich Stadium with sell out crowd on opening day in 1995 as seen from a helicopter being flown by Neil Lipke of Hamburg, NY with yours truly taking the photos.

Joe Ferguson #12 (1973-84) having his name placed on the Wall of Fame in Rich Stadium gets a handshake from Kent Hull #67.

Pregame festivities on the field as members of The Buffalo Bills Booster Club carry their banner off the field.

Players from the 60's: Daryle Lamonica #12 the QB and Pete Gogolak #3 our soccer style kicker.

Billy Shaw #66 made it onto the stadium's Wall of Fame. He played From 1961-69

SOME COLOR FROM THE PAST

A hectic time on the field at Rich Stadium as the Bills were nearing their first Super Bowl. Fans were celebrating a playoff victory.

O.J.Simpson #32 in action in the early 70's.

Thurman Thomas #34 on his way to a 1000-yard season in the 90's.

AND PRESENT

ABOVE: Believe it or not..We have a cemetery right in the middle of one of our parking lots on stadium property. Jeanne Smith looks over the unusual sight.

LEFT: Our leader in the 90's has been Jim Kelly #12 who took us to four straight Super Bowls.

One of our stars on the team has been Bruce Smith #78. This photo shows the intensity he has to GET THE QUARTERBACK.

Our **roller coaster ride** made only a slight move up as we won 3 and lost 11, keeping us mired in last place in the AFC East. Coach Jim Ringo worked on the assistant coaching positions and by mid-February had his full staff ready to go. Our first draft choice was Phil Dokes, and then came the likes of Curtis Brown, Charlie Romes, and kicker Neil O'Donoghue. On August 13 Jim Ringo got his first win as a coach and the entire team was elated. Miami defeated the Bills in the first game of 1978 and now held a 15 straight victory series. Our winless drought came to an end when we played Atlanta to a 3-0 score in front of our most poorly attended game in the history of The Bills with a crowd of 27,348. The shocker of the year happened when O.J. was injured in the Seattle game and was told he required knee surgery that would probably end his playing career. November 6 we won our second game of the year and on December 11 our third and last victory for 1977. The candidate list was out and Marv Levy was mentioned to replace Jim Ringo. But there was another coach headed in Buffalo's direction from the West Coast by the name of Chuck Knox.

Coach Jim Ringos first win as he is presented a game ball from O.J. Simpson.

Tony Greene #43 led the team with nine interceptions by the end of the season.

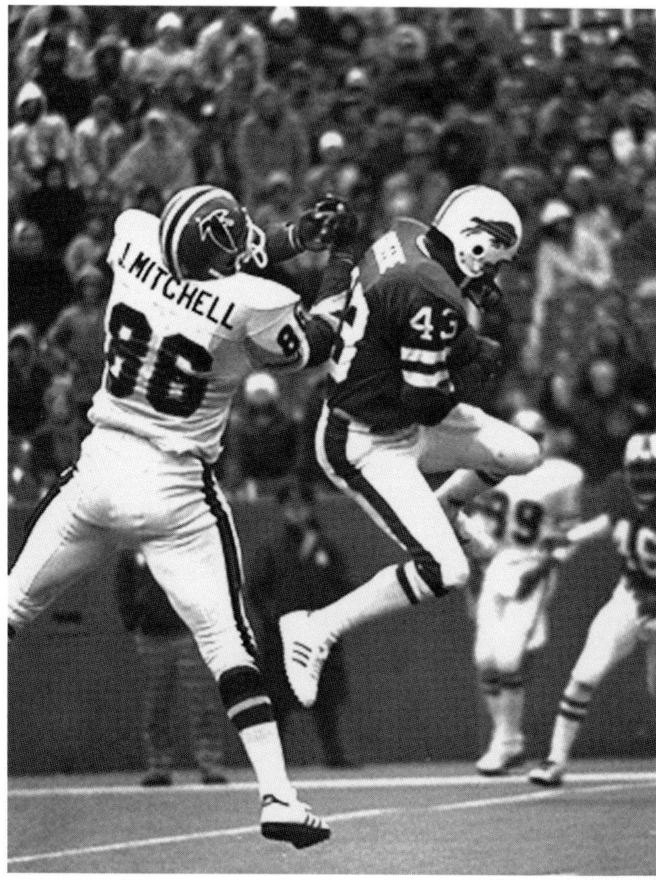

Our crowds in the '77 season were very sparse. Few were on hand to watch our new kicker Neil O'Donoghue #8.

O.J. Simpson #32 as he recorded his 10,000th yard when we played the Falcons.

1977

Brian Sipe #12, the QB of the Browns, under intense pressure.

Reuben Gant #88 proved to be a great receiver in a dismal year. Here he scores against the Falcons.

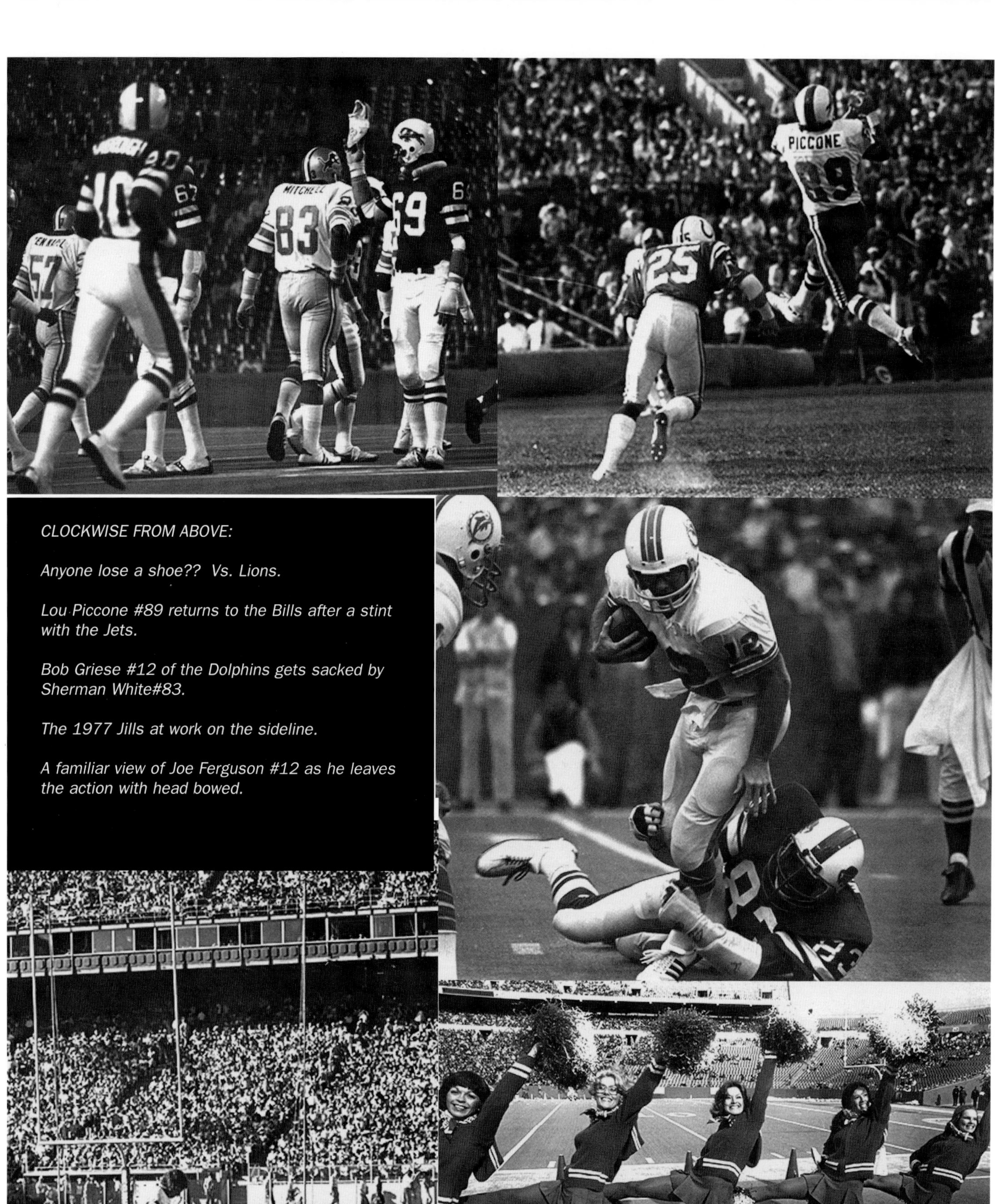

CLOCKWISE FROM ABOVE:

Anyone lose a shoe?? Vs. Lions.

Lou Piccone #89 returns to the Bills after a stint with the Jets.

Bob Griese #12 of the Dolphins gets sacked by Sherman White#83.

The 1977 Jills at work on the sideline.

A familiar view of Joe Ferguson #12 as he leaves the action with head bowed.

Another rare photo in a losing season...Left to right: Bobby Chandler #81, Lou Piccone #89, Joe Ferguson #12.

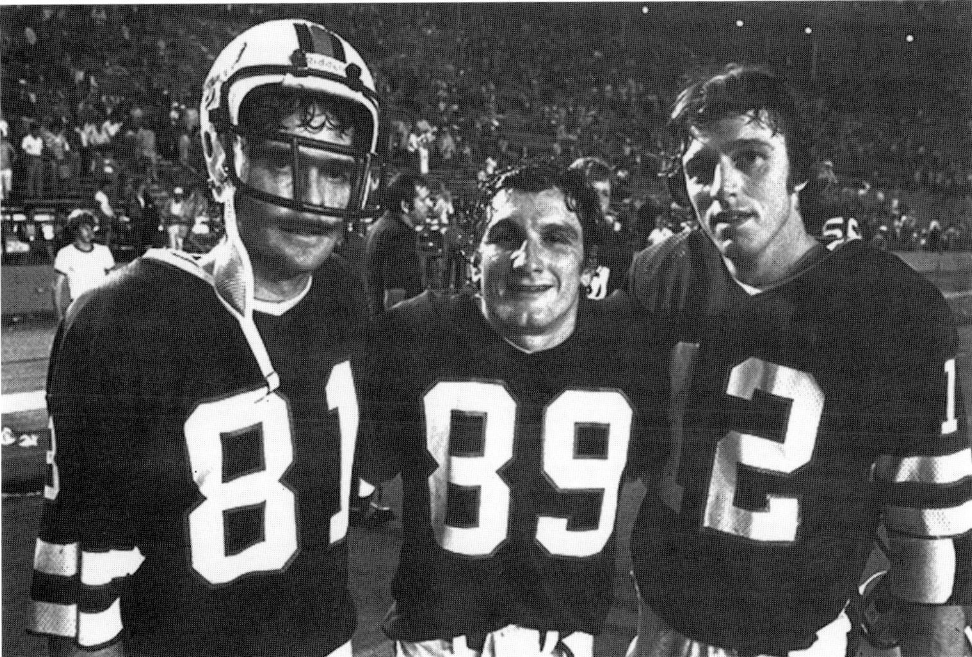

Jim Ringo's last game as Head Coach as he watches with Paul Seymour #87 along the sidelines.

Coach Knox gets his first win in Buffalo and gets a handshake from Joe Ferguson #12 and the game ball with a 24-17 over the Colts.

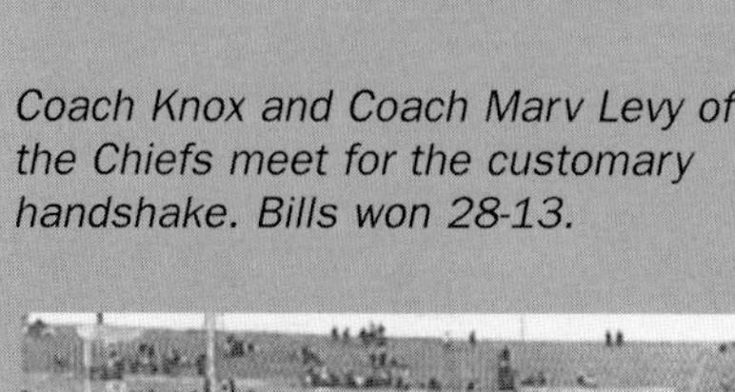

Coach Knox and Coach Marv Levy of the Chiefs meet for the customary handshake. Bills won 28-13.

Curtis Brown #47 on a long gainer vs. Jets.

Young fans display their love for #12, Joe Ferguson.

1978

The new year brought with it a new head coach by the name of Chuck Knox from the Los Angeles Rams, and with him came a very winning attitude. The **roller coaster** slowly moved along toward a fast rise—we would become the AFC East champions in three short years. We managed to win 5 and lose 11, but we were no longer at the bottom of the AFC East. Once again the assistant coaches were in a constant changeover, but the big news of the preseason was the trading of O.J. Simpson to San Francisco for a flock of draft choices. It was at this time that O.J. said,"I'll always be a Buffalo Bill and

A Buffalo Jills tryout.

I'm proud of that." Our first round in the draft went to select O.J.'s replacement, Terry Miller of Oklahoma State. Then came Scott Hutchinson, Dee Hardison, Lucious Sanford, and Will Grant. We then signed kicker Tom Dempsey, who holds the NFL record for the longest field goal of 63 yards. Prior to the season opener the Rolling Stones played in Rich Stadium before a crowd of 72,000. In August we acquired Bill Munson, a quarterback from San Diego, not to be mistaken with Bill Munson , the assistant general manager of the Bills organization. We started the season with 3 losses in a row, one of them being to the Dolphins for the 17th straight time. Later in the year the Dolphins made it 18 straight wins when we played in Buffalo. Coach Knox won his first game as the Bills' coach against the Colts, and it seemed as though the coaster was about to climb. With 5 wins we finally got out of the cellar and headed up.

The Buffalo Jills celebrate a win.

Tom Dempsey #6 hits from the 40 for a field goal.

Terry Miller #40 celebrates after scoring his first TD as a pro.

A happy Coach Knox hugs defensive player Sherman White #83 after a victory over the Bengals.

1978

Joe Ferguson #12 listens to the refs...Hey Joe, no listening!

Lou Piccone #89 celebrates a TD against the Giants.

Coach Knox celebrates the Bills' first road win in two years...vs. the Colts 21-14.

BUFFALO BILLS
BUFFALO BILLS
BU BI

1979

Stew Barber was elevated to general manager of the team , thus working his way up from the playing ranks of the Bills to the top post. Another of our former players, quarterback Tom Flores, was named head coach of the Oakland Raiders. In the draft we selected a player by the name of Tom Cousineau from Ohio State, then used our second #1 draft choice in selecting WR Jerry Butler. Later in the draft came Fred Smerlas, Jim Haslett, Jon Borchardt, Jeff Nixon, Rod Kush, and Dan Manucci. With 7 wins and 9 losses the **roller coaster** was gaining some speed to reach the top. A shocker took place when our first #1 draft choice, Tom Cousineau, signed with the Canadian Football League for less money than was offered by the Bills. We completed our second winless preseason and looked with apprehension toward the 1979 season. Tom Dempsey, our kicker, was waived after the first three games, and we brought onboard a fellow named Nick Mike-Mayer of the Eagles. Jerry Butler showed everyone his talent with a spectacular game vs. the Jets that had him catching 10 passes for 4 touchdowns and 255 yards. Also Joe Ferguson fired 5 TD passes against the Jets at Rich Stadium. The Dolphins completed a decade of wins over the Bills by defeating us twice in games #19 and #20. O.J. Simpson retired from football and became world famous as an actor and sports commentator. Joe Ferguson had a banner year but was overlooked for the AFC Pro Bowl team, even though he led the NFL in passing for eleven weeks. We were nearing the top of the ride but wouldn't reach it this year.

LEFT: Seven wins...the coaster moves up!

Sherman White #83 as he pursues the Jets QB.

Jerry Butler #80 vs. Jets with a banner day of 4 TDs and 255 yards.

After the Jets game the two heroes pose... Left to right: Joe Ferguson and Jerry Butler.

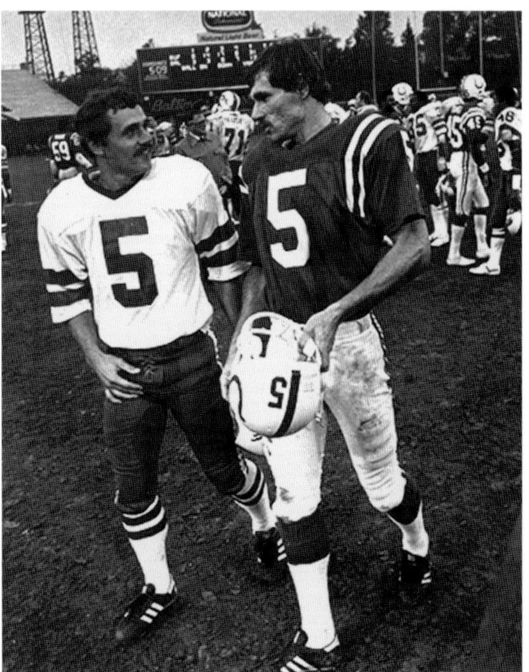

Two #5s who are brothers meet on the playing field: (left to right) Nick Mike-Mayer and brother Steve with the Colts.

Posing for publicity photos in their off-season jobs as bankers, (seated) Terry Miller and (standing) Lucious Sanford.

Bart Starr, head coach of the Packers, watches his team lose to the Bills, 19-12.

1979

A super fan of the Bills is Rev. Eugene Barrett of Lancaster Community Baptist Church, who met the plane at the airport on every departure and arrival.

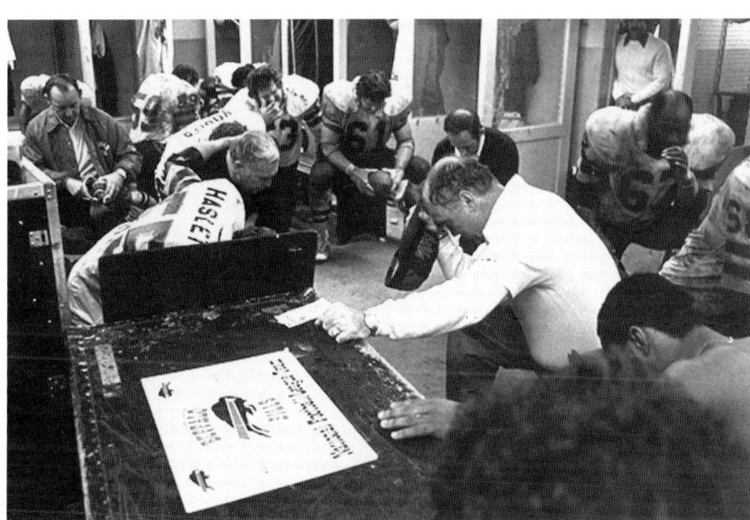

Dressing room after a game ... players stop to pray.

Snow...Fans will do anything to get to the game.

The era of Coach Knox was going strong and the **roller coaster** was once again nearing the top. We had 11 wins and 5 losses, bringing us to a AFC divisional playoff game against our old nemesis, the San Diego Chargers, only to lose 20-14. We traded a well-liked player, Bobby Chandler, for Phil Villapiano and in the draft added the names of Jim Ritcher, Joe Cribbs, Gene Bradley, Mark Brammer, Erwin Parker, and punter Greg Cater. Another player who arrived this year was the controversial Conrad Dobler from New Orleans. On September 20 the Bills finally beat Miami, ending a 20-game drought in front of one of our largest crowds—79,598. Fans stormed the field, tore down the goal posts, and actually passed one of the posts up to Ralph Wilson's private box. We won the first five games of the year, becoming the only team to win all their games up to that point. The fans were so happy that over 5,000 were at the airport to greet us when we came back from San Diego with our 5th win in a row. On December 7 we won a game vs. the Los Angeles Rams on a Nick Mike-Mayer field goal, a day that will go down in memory as the day the players came "back out" on the field after the game and danced for the fans. We won the AFC title in a mud game at Candlestick Park in San Francisco and were once again met by 8,000 fans in 14 degree weather at 4:00 in the morning. Now those are fans! The team traveled to Vero Beach, Florida, to practice for the playoff game, but to no avail. We were beaten by a guy named Dan Fouts, who threw a 50-yard touchdown pass with 2:08 remaining, as San Diego defeated the Bills 20-14. But **the coaster** was still poised on the top of the hill with another great year coming in 1981.

Players and friends surround Tony Marchetti when he retired as equipment manager of Bills.

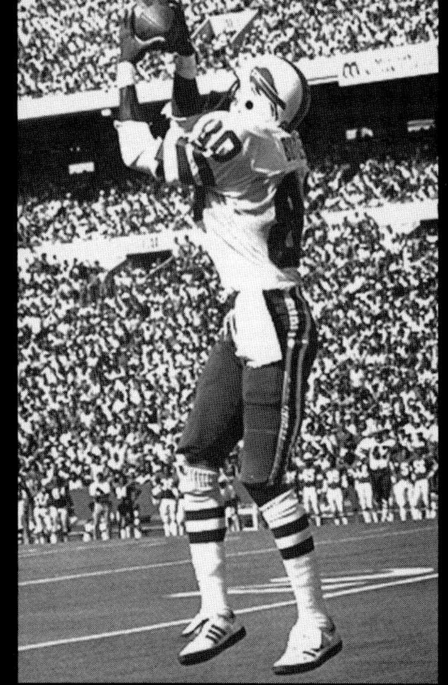

Jerry Butler for first down.

The aftermath as the Bills beat Miami first time in 20 games!

1980

The Bills win over Miami — down come the goalposts!

Bills sing their"We're Going to the Super Bowl" song after each victory.

Winning TD by Joe Cribbs #20 as he comes right to the camera for posterity ...vs. Patriots.

Dr. Steve Hudecki, the team dentist, takes a look at Charley Romes #26 after a play.

Game ball to Phil Villapiano #41 (an ex-Raider) after helping the defense limit the Raiders to 157 yards.

The crowd of fans at the airport greeting their heroes home after defeating the Chargers 26-24.

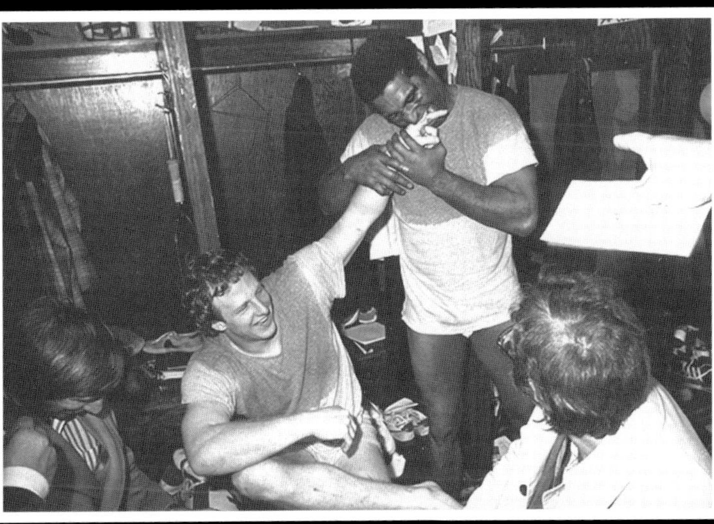

Jim Hasslett and Isiah Robertson reenact an altercation they had at a local pub that received media attention.

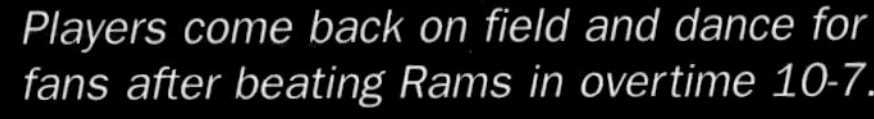

Players come back on field and dance for fans after beating Rams in overtime 10-7.

Mike Kadish #71 gets double-teamed vs. the Jets.

Joe Cribbs #20 with a TD reception as we win at Baltimore 35-3.

Mark Brammer #88 gets a TD reception vs. the Colts.

RIGHT: Conrad Dobler and Phil Villapiano dress in their pj's at a Bills' wives' function.

FAR RIGHT: Van Miller, the "Voice of the Bills," gets an interview with Ben Williams in the dressing room.

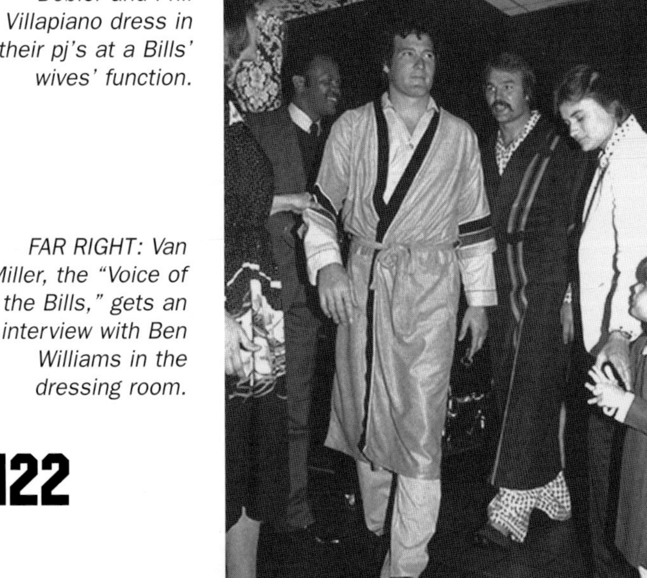

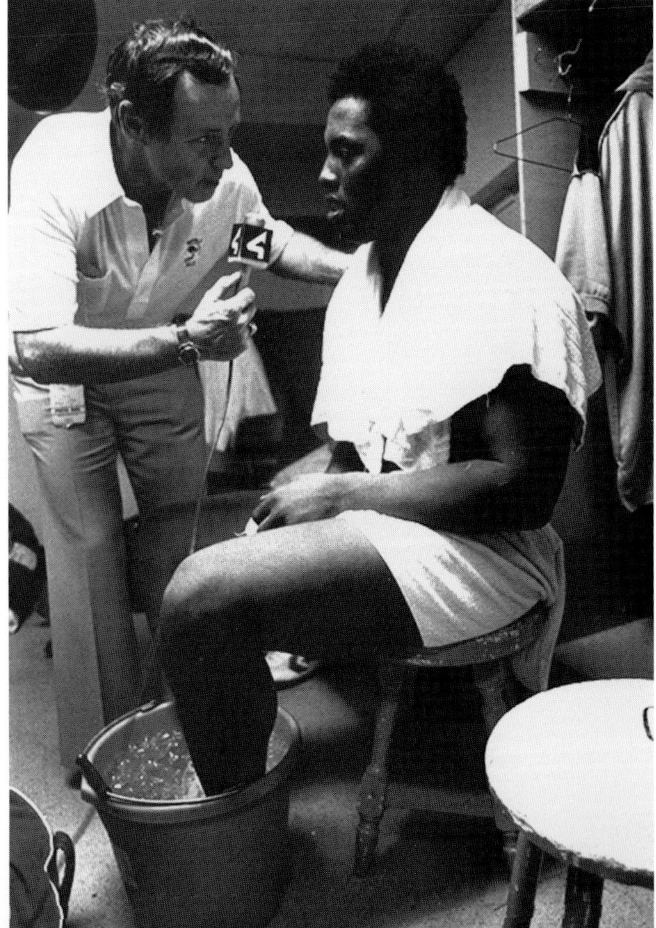

The **roller coaster** shot toward the top again...This was the year we won 10 and lost 6 to take third place in the AFC East. This record gave us a spot in the playoffs. We beat the Jets in the playoffs and then headed to River Front Stadium for the AFC Divisional Playoff, which we lost to the Bengals 28-21.The Bengals went on to Super Bowl XVI, only to lose to San Francisco. This was also the year our former coach, Jim Ringo, was inducted into the Pro Football Hall of Fame. We moved our training camp to Fredonia State College and the entire community of Fredonia was ecstatic. In the draft we traded places with Oakland and drafted Booker Moore first. Other picks this year were Chris Williams, Byron Franklin, Mike Mosley, Robert Geathers, Robb Riddick, and Justin Cross. The Erie County legislature replaced the turf at the stadium. As the season was about to start, the team cut Dan Manucci, Reuben Gant, and David Humm. Our opener against the Jets was superb as we handed them a 31-0 thrashing. Later in the season we lost our first overtime game in team history to Cincinnati 27-24. Conrad Dobler and Coach Knox got into a verbal argument on the sidelines and in the dressing room after the Dallas game on Monday Night Football. On November 22 the Bills beat the Patriots with a "Hail Mary" pass with 5 seconds left on the clock and very few fans left in the stadium to see the play. The regular season came to an end with the Bills earning a playoff spot. We beat the Jets in a Wildcard game, 31-27. Then lost to the Bengals in AFC Divisional Playoffs, 28-21.

Coach Chuck Knox shows his emotions late in the game with a win over Miami 31-21.

The fans are from Iroquois High School in Elma, N.Y.

Kicker Nick Mike-Mayer holds game ball after defeating Denver 9-7 with his kick. Photo by Tex Smith

Fred Smerlas #76 after QB Brian Sipe of the Browns.

The 1981 Buffalo Jills and Junior Jills.

1981

Bob Bukaty, a photographer from the Courier Express, shows how to take Florida pictures that show palm trees...you just bring along your own branch.

Hail Mary Pass caught by Roland Hooks #25 to beat Patriots with 5 seconds remaining.

Frank Lewis #82 scoring a TD vs. the Chiefs.

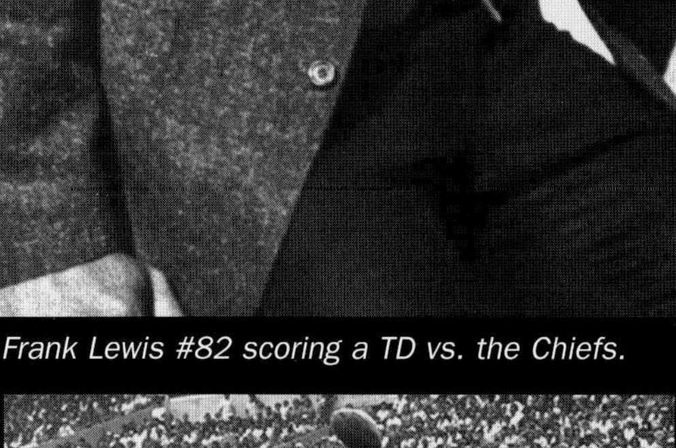

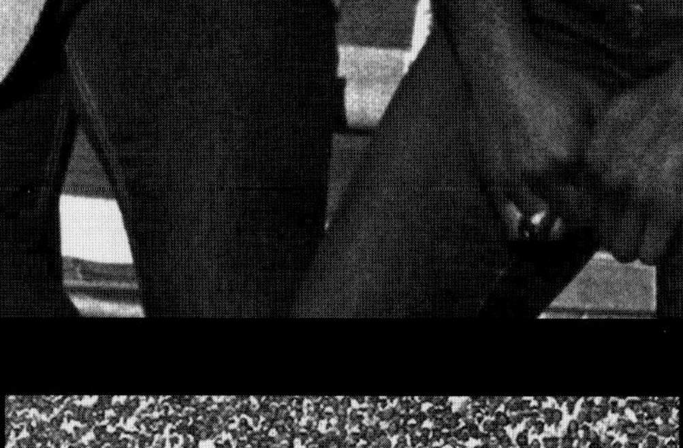

1982

This was the year of the 57-day players' strike. The **roller coaster** made a slight dip in the climb as we won 5 and lost 4 with the shortened season, and there was no playoff game in sight for the Bills. The Tom Cousineau matter came to a head with the Bills signing him, then trading him to the Browns for draft picks. Our number one in the draft was Perry Tuttle from Clemson, then Matt Kofler, Eugene Marve, Van Williams, and kicker Gary Anderson from Syracuse. Conrad Dobler was not invited back to camp. Mini-camp opened and Joe Cribbs was absent, as he was asking for a $1 million salary including signing bonus and benefits. The season started with a win over Coach Marv Levy's team, the Chiefs. Jerry Butler was coming to terms, Joe Cribbs was still a holdout, and we cut Mike Kadish. September 20 marked the start of the strike that would shorten the season to nine games. The teams would not play again until November 16. A very unhappy Joe Cribbs reported to camp but vowed he would be asking for a lot more money in 1983. Later in the season we held Pittsburgh to 94 yards, including a minus 2 yards passing for Terry Bradshaw. On December 28 we lost to Miami again, giving Coach Shula his 200th win as a head coach. We were eliminated from the playoffs by the Patriots in Massachusetts, making it three losses in a row on the road. Super Bowl XVII was won by Washington over the Miami Dolphins, and the Bills were once again taking a slow ride to the top of the next peak.

Three top draft choices meet with Coach Knox: (left to right) Eugene Marve, Matt Kofler, Perry Tuttle, and Coach Knox...at Rich Stadium.

An emotional moment on the Bills bench as we defeat the Vikings in Orchard Park, NY.

Our defense upends Curtis Dickey of the Colts for no yards gained for the day in a 20-0 blowout.

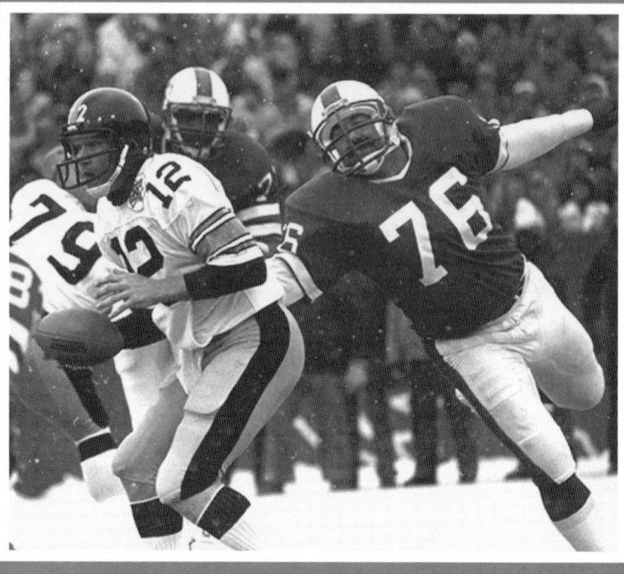

Terry Bradshaw #12 of the Steelers is about to meet Fred Smerlas #76 of the Bills for a sack.

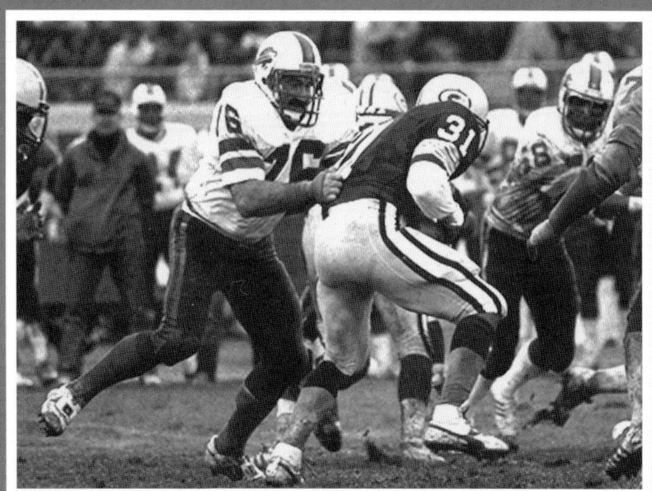

Fred Smerlas #76 shows how he started the game and how he looked at the end in a loss to the Packers in Wisconsin 33-21.

1982

At Jills reunion, Jane Delaney of Lancaster, N.Y., a cheerleader from 1975-77, looks at her old team photo. Jane has since passed away and will always be remembered by her teammates.

Photographers show the Jills a pose. I am doing the honors as Rob McElroy shoots.

Jerry Butler #80 is greeted by fans as he leaves the field after scoring the winning TD against the Vikings.

Jerry Butler #80 scores a TD against the Oilers as we win 30-13.

Top draft picks in town...Left to right: Tony Hunter, Daryl Talley, and Jim Kelly.

1983

Players carry Coach Stephenson off the field in Cincinnati after his first win as head coach.

Our ride on the **roller coaster** was anything but smooth. We hit quite a bump when Coach Knox resigned his position with the Bills to accept the head coaching spot with the Seattle Seahawks team. The players were upset with the coaching situation, but out of the all the names being mentioned, we signed Kay Stephenson at the top spot. Kay was a quarterback with the Bills during the 1968 season and vowed that the players would be behind him when the season started. With a new coaching staff, the Bills drafted TE Tony Hunter and Jim Kelly with their two first round choices. Then came Darryl Talley in the second round and Trey Junkin in the fourth round. The U.S. Football League started operating and caused some concern to the NFL clubs that had unsigned players. On June 9 Jim Kelly signed a contract with the USFL Houston Gamblers, and thus the Bills were put on Kelly's back burner. Harvey Johnson, a two-time head coach of the Bills, died of a heart attack at the age of 64. We started the season with a loss to Miami as they made four field goals and we missed three for a 12-0 score. On September 11 Coach Stephenson won his first game as head coach when we defeated the Bengals in Cincinnati 10-6. Soon after that, on October 5, we played Miami at home and they started a new QB by the name of Dan Marino. Miami finally lost at home to the Bills 38-35 in overtime with a field goal by the Bills' Joe Danelo. We won 8 games and lost 8 with a new head coach. The **coaster** had just started a bit of a climb, but we were headed for a big dive in 1984.

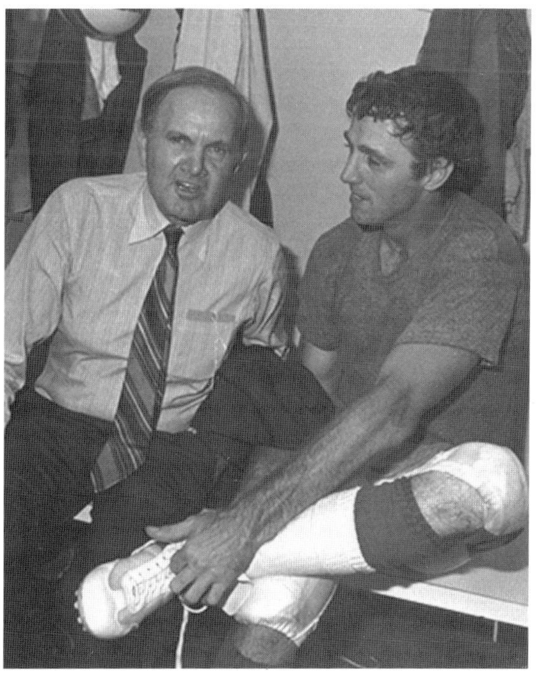

Ralph Wilson and Joe Ferguson at a happy moment after our first win vs. Miami since 1966.

Former Bills QBs, now Head Coaches, Kay Stephenson and Tom Flores of the Raiders. Raiders win 27-24.

New GM Terry Bledsoe on left with Ralph Wilson and Pat McGroder in Bills' front office area.

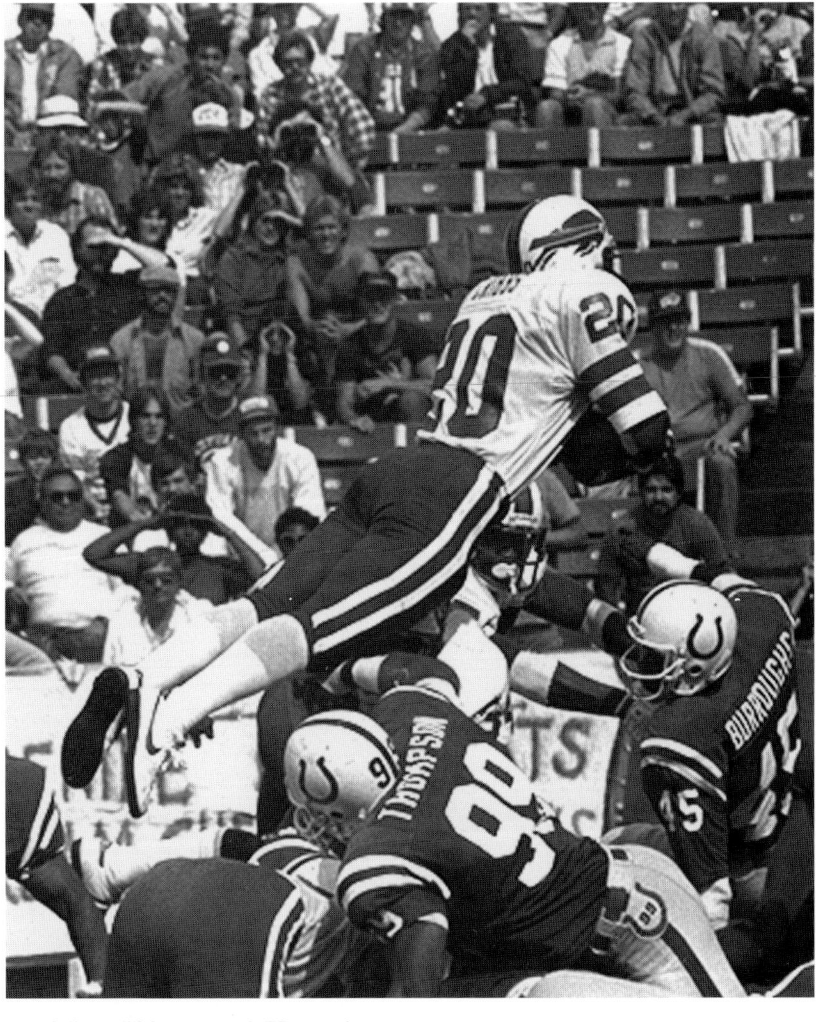

Joe Cribbs #20 scores 3 TDs and rushes for 82 yards, receiving 14 yards, in a win over the Colts.

ABOVE: (Left to right:) Joe Ferguson #12, Coach Frank Kush of the Colts, and Coach Kay Stephenson of the Bills as they walk off field with a Bills victory.

Rob Riddick #40 shows great form on this punt return vs. the Jets. We win 24-17.

Steve Freeman #22 expresses the feelings of the team on the last game of the year with no playoff in sight.

N.Y. Gov. Mario Cuomo visits the Bills' camp in Fredonia. This is only NFL team in N.Y. State.

Frank Woods, a photographer from Springbrook, N.Y., lets his feelings be known on this play when Miami was in town.

What a year for the Bills! We lost 14 and won only 2 games with the **roller coaster** once again heading for the bottom. Our new general manager was Terry Bledsoe, Joe Cribbs was now in the USFL, Jim Speros was our first strength coach, and the Baltimore Colts moved their team to Indianapolis in the middle of the night. A bright spot this year was the naming of our Silver Anniversary Team and the unveiling of our new helmet logo. Our top draft choice was Greg Bell to replace Joe Cribbs, who had just won the rushing title with 1,467 yards in the USFL. Unnoticed was the hiring of Bill Polian as director of pro personnel, a person who would go on to become extremely important to the Bills franchise in the future. We started the season off with 11 straight losses and the fans crying for Coach Stephenson's head. The team responded with a stunning victory over the Dallas Cowboys, our first win of the year. We were to win only one more game that year. Joe Ferguson was benched, and a new quarterback, Joe Dufek, was slated to start against the Colts. Thus ended Ferguson's streak of continuous starts. With our losses at 12, we were once again the owners of the first draft choice for 1985, and a fellow by the name of Bruce Smith was waiting. Our downward plunge had hit the bottom, and we thought we were about to start climbing again. This proved to be wrong.

1984

What do you do when you lose? You clip your nails. Will Grant #53.

Coach Stephenson suffers one loss after another... Can the end be far away?

Jack Kemp was installed on the Wall of Fame on November 18.

Joe Dufek #15 starting in place of Joe Ferguson, hands off to Greg Bell #28.

Our first win after 11 losses, and we carry Coach Stephenson off the field in Orchard Park, NY.

1984

25-year reunion at steps to City Hall in Buffalo. Left to right: Mayor Jim Griffin, Ralph Wilson, County Executive Ed Rutkowski (former player), and Paul Maguire #55. Others (standing left to right): Tom Sestak #70, Stew Barber #77, Ron McDole #72, Billy Shaw #66, Mike Stratton #58, Al Bemiller #50, Butch Byrd #42.

Jim Ritcher #51 shows the feelings of winning 2 and losing 12.

Kay Stephenson with Coach Knox, now with the Seahawks.

We remained at the bottom of the **roller coaster** ride with another 2-12 season, tied for last place in the league with Tampa Bay. Coach Kay Stephenson was given the green light for the season from Ralph Wilson, but five of his assistant coaches left the team. Hank Bullough was hired as a defensive coordinator and assistant head coach. O.J. Simpson was named to the Pro Football Hall of Fame, becoming the first Buffalo Bills player to be so honored. Jim Ringo returned to the coaching ranks as offensive coordinator and offensive line coach. Bill Polian and Norm Pollom replaced Terry Bledsoe, the general manager, who suffered a heart attack. Bruce Smith became our first draft choice and we promptly signed him to a four-year, multi-million-dollar contract. We also drafted Derrick Burroughs, Mark Traynowicz, Chris Burkett, Frank Reich, Hal Garner, and Andre Reed. Tony Marchitte, who had been the equipment manager for nineteen years, died of cancer. We traded Tony Hunter to the Rams for Vince Ferragamo, a quarterback. We then sent Byron Franklin to Seattle for Pete Metzelaars. Joe DeLamielleure came back to the Bills, and this was the year we honored the 1964-65 champions. Patrick McGroder was placed on the Wall of Fame, and Coach Stephenson was fired after losing the first four games of the year. Hank Bullough was named head coach but the **roller coaster** stayed at the bottom of the dip.

After Tony Marchitte died, a chair was placed on the spot where he sat after his retirement from the Bills.

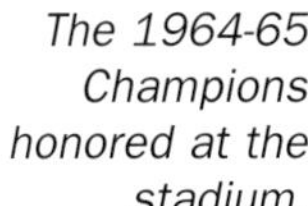

The 1964-65 Champions honored at the stadium.

1985

Scott Norwood #11 on the dressing room floor at half-time. What will the second half bring?

Patrick McGroder holding one of his grandchildren on the day his name is installed on the Wall of Fame.

Coach Kay Stephenson's last game as head caoch vs. Minnesota 27-20. He was fired the next day.

New head coach Hank Bullough seems to be knighting Darryl Talley #56.

Hank Bullough's first win as head coach, vs. Colts 21-9 on October 20.

A game ball was given to Coach Hank Bullough after his first victory as a head coach.

General Manager Bill Polian and New York Governor Mario Cuomo at a luncheon to welcome the governor to Buffalo.

Hank Bullough started his first full year as head coach and the **roller coaster** was poised at the bottom of the hill waiting for an upward drive. The assistant coaches were still being shuffled in and out of Buffalo. We drafted Ronnie Harmon of Iowa as our first #l pick and Will Wolford of Vanderbilt our second pick, in the first round. Then came Leonard Burton, Carl Byrum, Mark Pike, and Butch Rolle. Public relations director L. Budd Thalman departed to Penn State and Denny Lynch was hired to replace him.

Patrick McGroder, the Bills' senior executive vice-president, died after a short illness, and Jim Braxton, a former fullback, died of cancer. The USFL was on a downward slide as they won their anti-trust suit against the NFL and were awarded a one-dollar settlement, which was later trebled to three dollars. Jim Kelly was given the green light to sign an NFL contract and thus became a Buffalo Bill with a five-year, $8 million contract. This thrust him into top pay in the NFL. When Kelly arrived in Buffalo he was given a hero's welcome that was attended by Governor Mario Cuomo. Kelly made his debut against the Jets but lost 28-24. Hank Bullough was replaced by Marv Levy of the Kansas City Chiefs when our record was 2-5. Steve Tasker was added to the roster in November and he also became a key to Marv Levy's success. Bill Polian was now the general manager and three of the key people—Kelly, Levy, and Polian—were on board as the **roller coaster** started on a great climb with 4 wins and 12 losses.

1986

Jim Kelly is given a hero's welcome to Buffalo. His Mom and Dad were proud parents as they listened to their son, a new Buffalo Bill.

Jim Kelly #12 ends up under the bench being looked over by Woody Ribbick, the assistant equipment man. Kelly was being chased and dove under bench.

Jim Kelly #12 is welcomed to his first regular season game in the NFL vs. the Jets.

Steve Freeman #22 gets a ball for playing in his 169th game, setting a Bills record on Sept. 28.

Ralph Wilson was awarded a game ball in the dressing room after we beat the Cardinals.

The woes of coaching...Bullough loses again. The end is near as he watches the Jets kick a field goal with 57 seconds left in game.

1986

New head coach Marv Levy gets his first win over the Pittsburgh Steelers 16-12

Derrick Burroughs #29 shows what a losing season looks like.

Kelly gets ready to pose for his poster in downtown Buffalo. It was called "Machine Gun Kelly."

1987

The Counterfeit Bills played to sparse crowds. This was their first game, vs. Colts.

The **roller coaster** started a long steady climb this year as we won 7 and lost 8. Marv Levy was getting his coaching staff in order and we drafted Shane Conlan as our first pick. Then came Nate Odomes, Roland Mitchell, Jamie Mueller, Leon Seals, Keith McKeller, and Howard Ballard. Jim Kelly wore clothes of the 1920s to pose for a poster of himself called "Machine Gun Kelly." A strike was in the future since the players seemed far apart from the owners on their contracts. The owners vowed that all games would be played with athletes brought in during the strike. We played the first two games of the year and then the players struck as promised. Players like Jim Kelly were losing about $100,000 per week during the strike. All games were canceled the first week, but after that the teams fielded were known as "counterfeit" players. They played two games before the strike was finally called off. The Counterfeit Bills played a very important game vs. the Jets and won in overtime, thus enabling the Bills to come close to the playoffs later in the year. The Bills made one of their biggest trades in mid-season as they gave up future draft choices along with player Greg Bell to the Colts for Cornelius Bennett. Three old-time players from the Bills died during this year, Tom Sestak, John Leypoldt, and Dudley Meredith. Tom Sestak's name was later placed on the Wall of Fame in the stadium. Super Bowl XXII was won by Washington over Denver. We were on a steady climb upward and soon would be at the top...but not next year.

Third Counterfeit Bills game and we win by this FG in overtime 6-3 over Giants. This is Todd Schlopy #3 kicking barefoot.

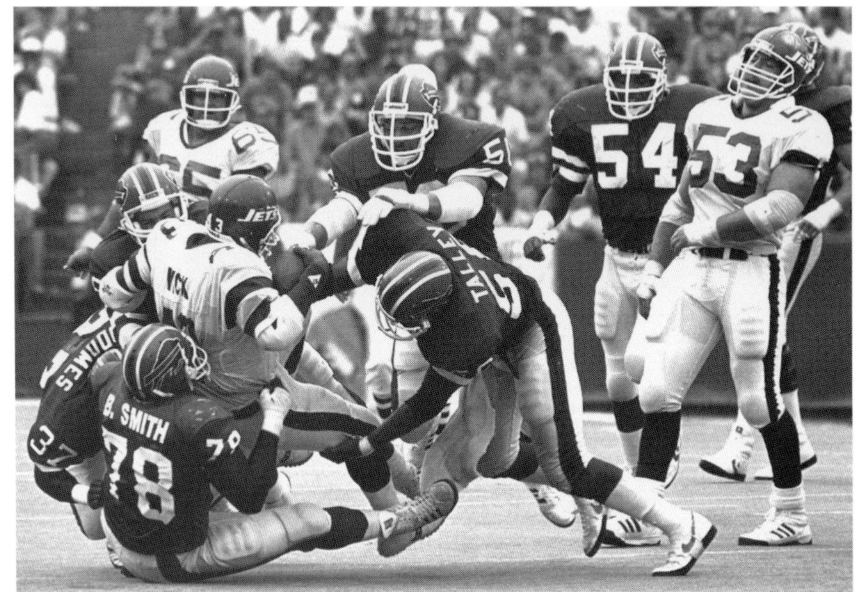

Our defense takes good care of Jets' runner Roger Vick as he gains a total of 34 yards for the day, but we lose 31-28.

Fans and friends celebrate Tom Sestak's name being placed on the Wall of Fame in the stadium.

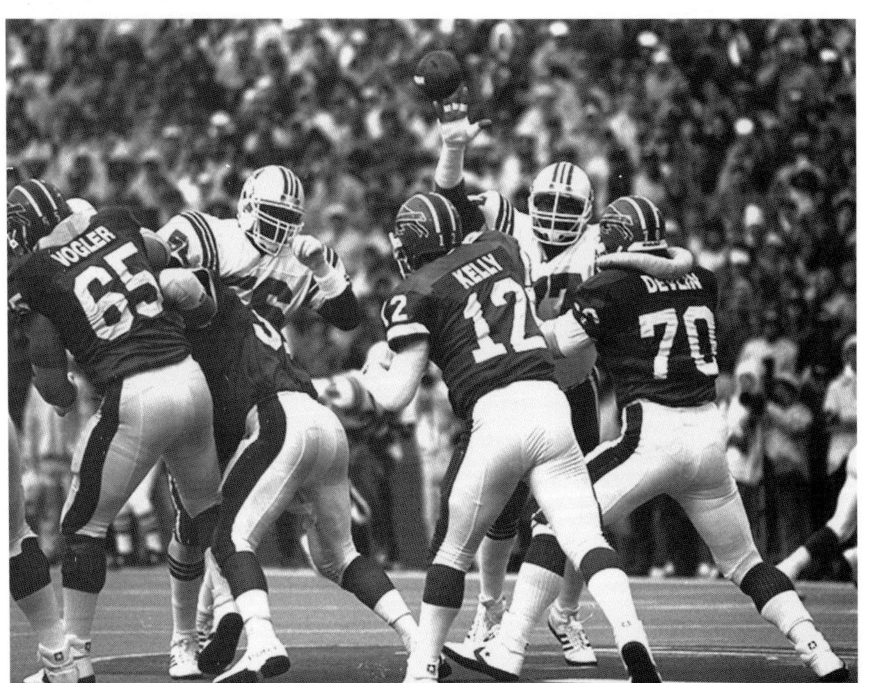

Jim Kelly #12 has his worst day as a pro in this loss to the Patriots, completing fewer than 50% of his passes. We lose to the Patriots 13-7.

Jamie Mueller #39 flies over the line for a first down vs. Miami.

Last game of the year as Bills' Tony Furjanic #53 brings down Bobby Morse of the Eagles.

How cold does it get when you're losing? Cold enough to put gloves on your feet.

Historic day in Buffalo Country as Thurman Thomas #34 scores his first TD as a Bill vs. the Vikings.

1988

Jim Kelly #12 and John Kidd #4 celebrate a close victory over the Dolphins 9-6.

The **roller coaster** gained speed and headed toward the top as the Bills won 12 and lost 4. We reached the playoffs and then the AFC Championship game, only to lose on a bid to go to the Super Bowl, being beaten by the Bengals 21-10 in Cincinnati. Our first pick of the draft was Thurman Thomas from Oklahoma State, who was selected on the 40th choice overall since we had no pick in the first round. Our second pick was Bernard Ford, a receiver from Central Florida. Fred Smerlas, Joe Devlin, and Jim Ritcher all signed new contracts, and Jerry Butler retired from football. Bruce Smith missed the first four games of the regular season. We won the first 4 games of the season and were on quite a roll, until we met Chicago in a 24-3 loss, with the Bills getting zero yards rushing. Scott Norwood was having a great year with field goals, setting a new record with 12 consecutive goals. On November 20 we clinched our first AFC East title since 1980 and the fans poured onto the field tearing down the goal posts. Ralph Wilson was elated that his team had gone from 4-12 to championship caliber in two years. On January 1 we beat Houston17-10 for the chance to win the AFC Championship in Cincinnati. We lost, and the Bengals went on to Super Bowl XXIII, only to be beaten by the 49ers 20-16. Our ride was close to the top, but we still had two years to wait.

Billy Shaw (1961-69) as his name is installed on the stadium Wall of Fame.

A pep rally for the team was held in downtown Buffalo prior to their game against the Oilers for the playoff game. We won that game 17-10.

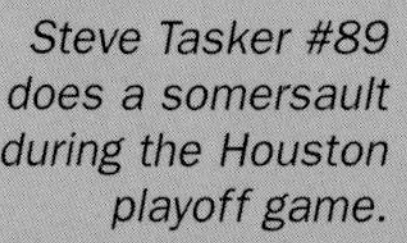

Steve Tasker #89 does a somersault during the Houston playoff game.

Goal Posts end up in seats after our win over the Jets and Bills winning AFC East title 9-6.

Fred Smerlas #76 brings down Doug Flutie of the Patrtiots.

1988

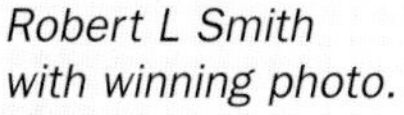

Robert L Smith
with winning photo.

Scott Norwood #11 after kicking winning field goal over Jets. That's Jim Ritcher #51 with arms outstretched. This photo won first place in the NFL for black & white action for 1988.

Ralph Wilson's name is installed on the Wall of Fame in the stadium. With the Wilson family is former Buffalo NY mayor James D. Griffin.

Joe Traver, a local photographer, uses some ingenuity as he photographs the crowd.

The **roller coaster** took a bit of a turn this year as we won 9 and lost 7. We still made the playoffs, only to lose to the Browns 43-30 in a thriller at Cleveland Stadium. Jim Ringo, one of the Bills' assistant coaches and former head coach, retired due to an injury he received in 1987. Bruce Smith signed a $7.5 million contract with the Bills for five years. With our first choices in the first and second rounds of the pick being traded away, we were not able to pick until the third round and drafted Don Beebe as the 82nd player selected in the draft. Other players selected by the Bills were Brian Jordan, Chris Hale, and Richard Harvey. This was the year that Dallas selected Troy Aikman as the first player overall in the draft. John Butler was named director of player personnel, and Bill Polian was given a contract through the 1992 season. In our season opener in Miami we beat the Dolphins in a thriller, as Jim Kelly dove into the end zone with no time left on the clock and scored his first NFL rushing touchdown in 45 games. James Lofton was signed as a free agent from the Raiders, and Greg Bell returned to play against the Bills. Frank Reich rallied the Bills in the 4th quarter against the unbeaten Rams in a Monday Night Football Game. It was a thrilling win in the last 16 seconds of the game and held Greg Bell to 44 yards rushing. On October 29 the Bills defeated Miami 30-17 in front of a record crowd of 80,208. Dan Marino was sacked for the first time in a record-breaking string of 19 games and 759 passing attempts. Phil Dokes, our first-round draft choice in 1977, died of heart failure at age 34. We clinched the AFC East division title, pounding the Jets 37-0, but lost to the Browns in Cleveland in the playoffs. Super Bowl XXIV was won by San Francisco over Denver, but look out! The Bills' **coaster** was shooting toward the top.

Don Beebe #82 gets upended as we play the Browns and lose in playoffs 34-30.

1989

The interception aftermath as Browns defeat the Bills 34-30 to win divisional playoff game.

Mark Kelso #38 puts in eye drops during a game.

Jim Kelly #12 talks to the troops during a loss to the Broncos.

Jeff Wright #91 sacks Marino. Marino had gone 19 games without being sacked.

1989

Cornelius Bennett #55 and a few others lend a hand to stop Eric Dickerson #29 of the Colts.

Andre Reed #83 catches one of his 4 receptions that totaled 114 yards vs. the Patriots.

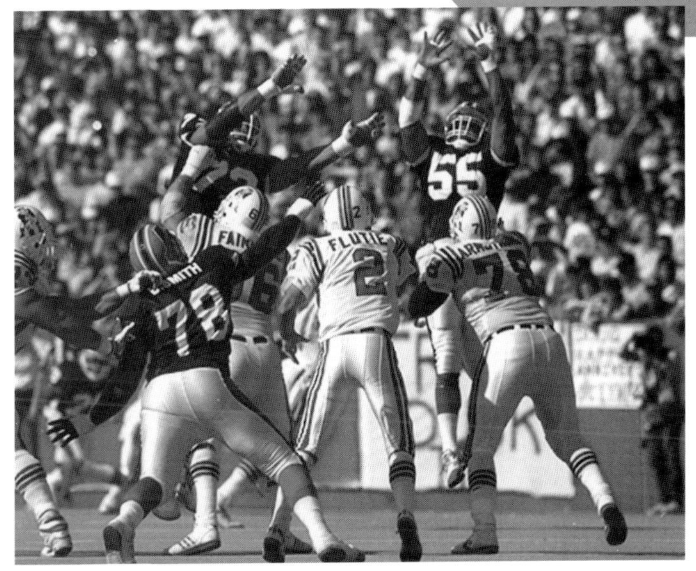

Doug Flutie of the Patriots has Bills' defenders all over him in this game; the Bills win 31-10.

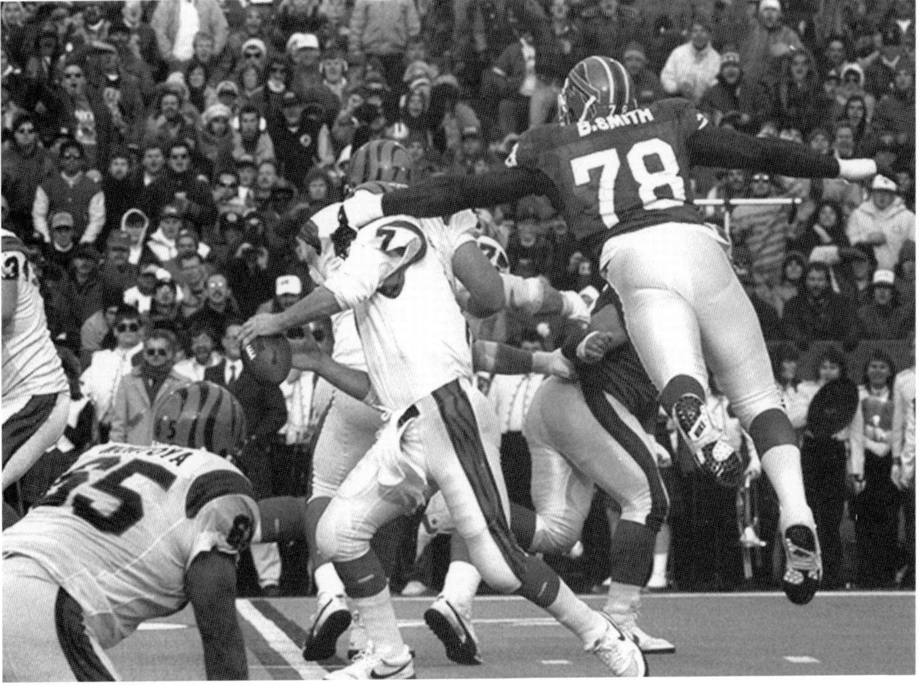

A flying Bruce Smith #78 as he reaches for Boomer Esiason #7 of the Bengals for a sack.

It took thirty-one years, but the Bills were about to ride the **roller coaster** to the very top as we headed for the Super Bowl for the first time. Jim Kelly became the highest paid player in the NFL with a $3-million-plus per year contract for seven years. Fred Smerlas signed with the San Francisco team, thus ending an eleven-year career with the Bills. J.D. Williams became our first selection in this year's draft, then Carwell Garner, Glenn Parker, Eddie Fuller, Marvcus Patton, and Mike Lodish. We started the season off with a win, then lost to Miami but followed that up with 8 victories before losing to Houston on November 26. The team had been named the "Bickering Bills" due to the inappropriate remarks that some players were making to the press about each other. Marv Levy successfully stopped the "bickering" and the Bills then won 8 straight games. The no-huddle offense was put into play and caused quite a stir among the other teams in the league. We clinched our third straight AFC East division title under the direction of Frank Reich, as Kelly was injured. We ended the regular season with 13 wins and 3 losses. In the playoff game we defeated Miami and then defeated the Raiders 51-3 in Buffalo. At last we were off to our first Super Bowl! The Persian Gulf war was raging in the Middle East, and Super Bowl XXV became a great diversion for the troops to watch on Super Sunday. With the score at 20-19 in favor of the Giants, Scott Norwood attempted a field goal with eight seconds left on the clock, missed, and the closest Super Bowl game in history came to a close with the Bills losing the game but not their fans. The following day a crowd of 20,000 attended a rally for the Bills, with fans chanting "We want Scott!" Norwood took the mike to speak to the people and dedicated 1991 to them. There was not a dry eye in the crowd.

Butch Rolle #87 scores the Bills' 1,000th TD in team history; vs. Colts.

Comeback Game: Bruce Smith #78 sacks John Elway #7 of the Broncos in a thriller 29-28.

Jim Kelly #12 runs for a first down vs. the Jets.

Andre Reed #83 scores. Celebrating players drop Reed (oops!).

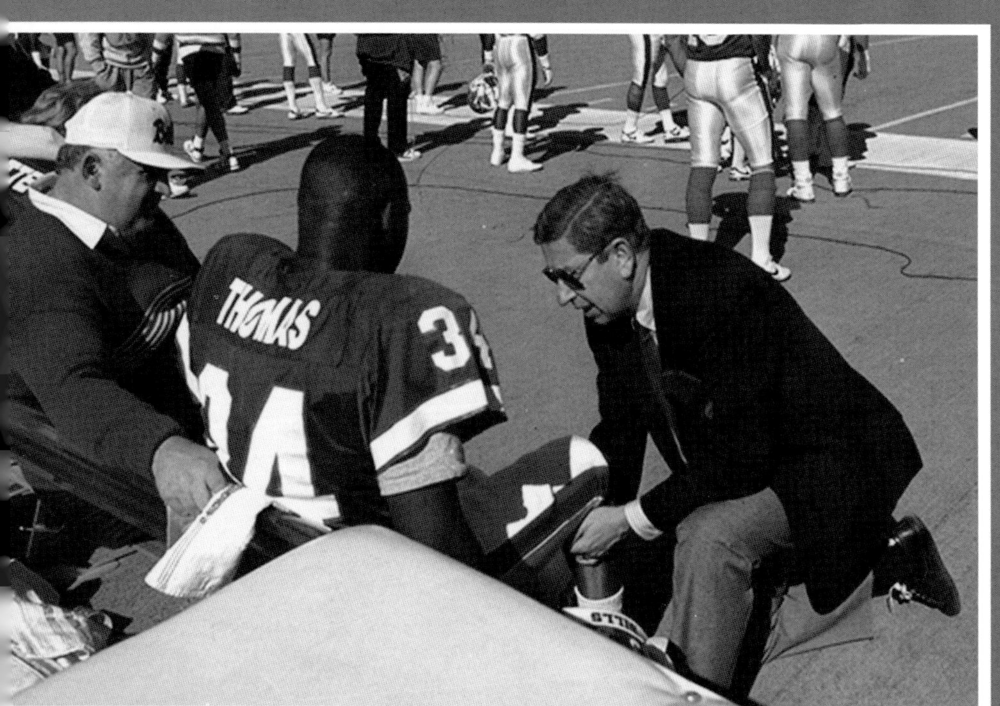

Dr. Richard Weiss on the sidelines working on Thurman Thomas #34.

No modesty on the sidelines as John Davis #65 drops his pants in front of 80,000 fans.

1990

J.D. Williams #31, our first draft choice, gets congrats after his first interception as a pro vs. the Patriots.

A game ball to Al Wheeler of Cheektowaga, N.Y. who was honored on the sidelines for being the Bills' driver for 25 years. He is the one who delivers their equipment to and from the airports.

Playoff game vs. Miami, January 12. We win to go against the Raiders next.

SUPER BOWL XXV

VS. THE NEW YORK GIANTS • TAMPA, FLORIDA • JANUARY 21, 1991
GIANTS 20/ BILLS 19

A safety is scored by Bills as we tackle Giants' QB Jeff Hostetler in end zone for 2 points.

Mitch Frerotte #59 with his war paint on for the "Game of Games."

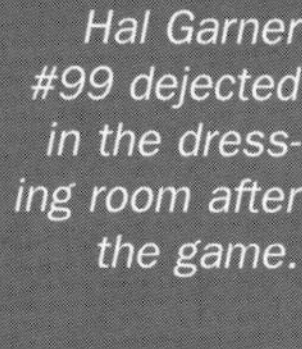

Hal Garner #99 dejected in the dressing room after the game.

1990

Post Super Bowl Rally in Buffalo. Scott Norwood addresses crowd telling them how sorry he is for the loss. There's not a dry eye in the group.

Politicians and team members listen as Ralph Wilson addresses the crowd outside City Hall in Buffalo NY.

Jim Kelly #12 and Thurman Thomas #34 pose for press photos at stadium.

Coach Levy checks the time for our next trip to the Super Bowl.

The stadium was packed for the Miami game.

1991

What a great season we had last year, and the **roller coaster** rolled along the top again this year as we made it to Super Bowl XXVI. Early in the year the turf at the stadium was replaced, and small parcels of the old turf were sold as Bills memorabilia. Henry Jones of Illinois became our first draft choice. We also selected Phil Hansen, Darryl Wren, and Mark Maddox. In July the Bills departed for London, England, to play the Eagles in the American Bowl game. We defeated the Eagles 17-13 in Wembley Stadium in front of 50,000 spectators. In August former Bill Paul Maguire suffered a heart attack and was listed as critical in Buffalo General Hospital. We won our season opener over Miami and had now won our last 9 out of 10 meetings with the Dolphins. We won our first 5 games of the season and ended the regular season with 13 wins and 3 losses, clinching the fourth straight AFC East division title by December 1. We defeated Kansas City in the playoff game, and then our win over the Denver Broncos propelled us to the top of the **coaster** ride and into Super Bowl XXVI. The game was played on January 26 at the Metrodome in Minneapolis, with the Bills once again coming away without the golden ring as the Washington Redskins win 37-24.

Steelers game as Andre Reed #83 caught his 400th pass and Don Beebe #82 tied a club record with four receiving TDs.

Joe Ferguson (1974-84) received the Distinguished Service Award in pregame ceremonies. Players congratulate him.

Pete Metzelaars #88 scores a TD vs. the Bengals as we win 35-16.

Paul Maguire (Bills player 1964-70), now an announcer, prior to the game has fun with the visiting band.

AFC Championship game. Play of the game. Carlton Bailey #54 ends up with a tipped pass and scores.

Jim Kelly #12 has balloons to contend with but still completes 14 out of 28 for 237 yards.

A happy Bruce Smith #78 leaves the field with a team victory over the Jets.

SUPER BOWL XXVI

VS. THE WASHINGTON REDSKINS • IN MINNEAPOLIS, MN. • JANUARY 26, 1992
REDSKINS 37/ BILLS 24

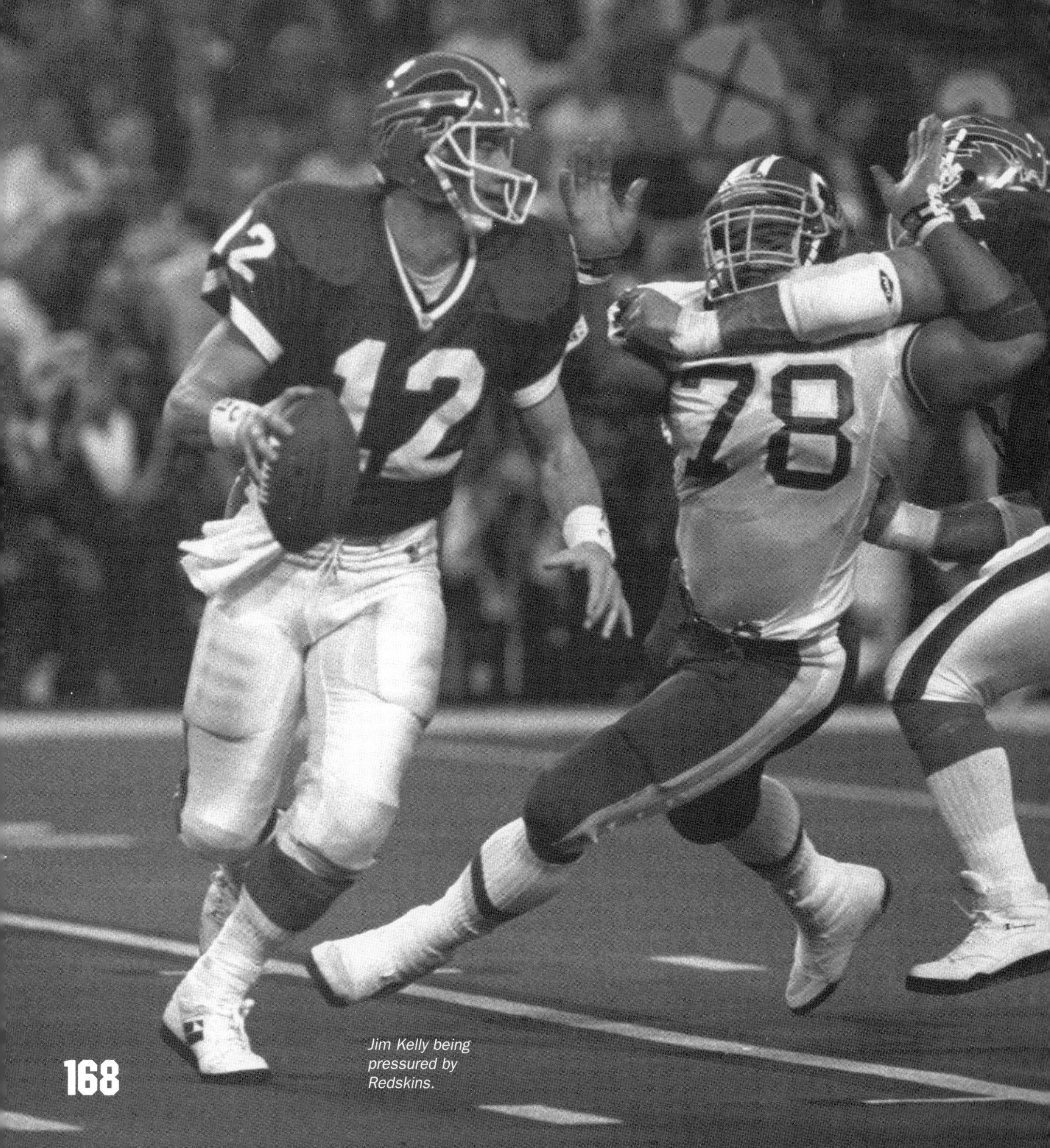

Jim Kelly being pressured by Redskins.

1991

Jim Kelly looks on in amazement as a second Superbowl slips away.

Rally in downtown Buffalo after Super Bowl XXVI. Ralph Wilson, team owner, addresses the crowd.

Niagara Square in Buffalo was the place to be when the fans of the Bills welcomed their team back after the Super Bowl. Our **roller coaster** was still teetering at the top, just waiting for that one extra nudge to reach the golden ring. This was the year in which we reached the Super Bowl with only 11 wins and 5 losses. We signed a new kicker named Steve Christie and waived Scott Norwood, ending his Buffalo career with 670 points. John Fina became our first draft choice, then James Patton, Keith Goganious, Matt Darby, Nate Turner, and Kurt Schulz. Once again we started the season off with four wins in a row, then two losses. We renewed our season with victories in the next five games, and along the way Marv Levy won his 71st victory as a Bills coach, making him the all-time leader of wins in the Bills franchise. In mid-December we played our 500th game in Bills history and it was a win over the Saints 20-16. Our loss to the Oilers cost us our fifth consecutive AFC East title, but later in the year we did go into the AFC Wildcard Playoff game and came away with a win over Houston in what is known as the "Miracle at Rich" game. Houston was leading in the third period by 35-3 but lost in overtime 41-38. We beat the Steelers 24-3 for the AFC Divisional Playoff and went to Florida where we once again beat the Dolphins for the AFC Championship. So here we were on top in the coaster and going into Super Bowl XXVII against the Cowboys in the Rose Bowl in California. We lost to the Cowboys 52-17 and became the first team

Magic Johnson of the NBA visits the sidelines of the Bills and ends up with the Jills.

1992

James Lofton #80 became the NFL all-time leader in receiving yardage as we played the Rams.

The 12th Man is installed on the Wall of Fame in the stadium. These folks represent the l2th Man.

In shutting out the Colts 38-0 the Bills' Steve Christie #2 kicks a 52-yard field goal.

Fans in the audience include Al Bemiller (wearing scarf) from 1961-69 teams.

"The Miracle Game:" The Bills Greatest comeback victory:
From a deficit of 35-3, the Bills won in overtime 41-38.

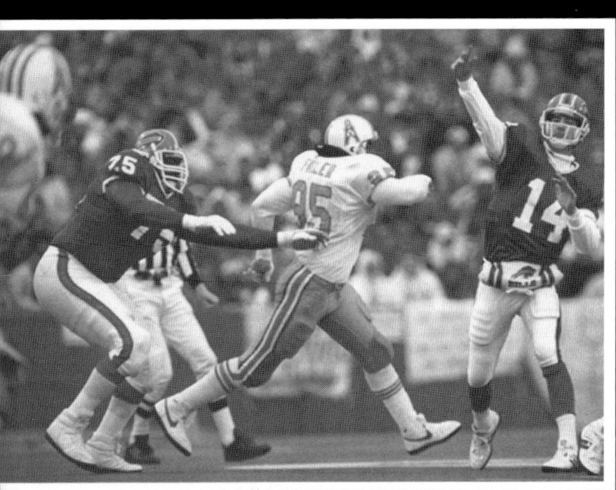

Frank Reich #14 completes 21 passes.

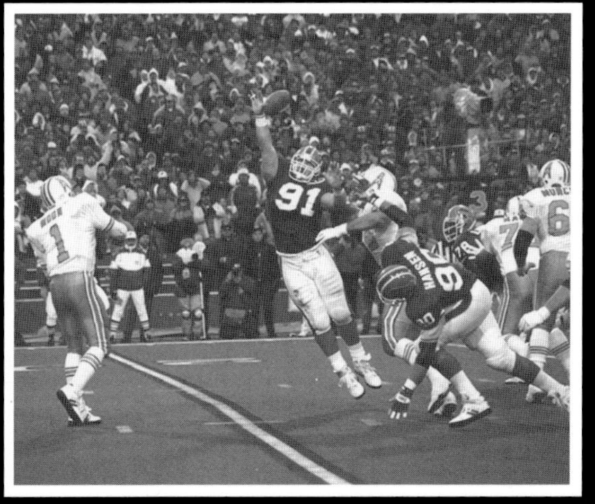

QB Warren Moon was under intense pressure.

Nate Odomes #27 intercepts the ball...

1992

...enabling the Bills to kick the winning field goal in overtime.

Jim Kelly
#12

SUPER BOWL XXVII

VS. DALLAS COWBOYS • IN PASADENA, CA • JANUARY 31, 1993
COWBOYS 52/ BILLS 17

A disbelieving Coach Levy watches his 3rd Super Bowl disappear as Dallas routs the Bills 52-17.

Don Beebe #82 had 2 receptions for 50 yards.

Thurman Thomas #34 held to 19 yards in Dallas victory 52-17.

1992

This was the year that the Bills scored 12 wins and 4 losses, with the **roller coaster** still poised at the top awaiting that final push to not only get to Super Bowl XXVIII but to win it. To start the year off, Bill Polian was fired as the Bills' general manager and was replaced by the likable John Butler. Jeff Wright and Will Wolford were named the Bills' transition players, meaning that we had to match any offer made to these players by other teams or lose them to that team. As a result we lost Will Wolford to the Colts, Shane Conlan to the Rams, and Mitch Frerotte to the Seahawks. The draft brought Thomas Smith as our first pick and then John Parrella and Russell Copeland. A newly created position, director of player relations and alumni, went to Jerry Butler, who played for the Bills from 1979-83. Thurman Thomas became the highest paid running back in the NFL when he signed a $13.5 million contract extension, keeping him as a Buffalo Bill for the remainder of his career. The Bills departed for Germany, where they played the Vikings in the American Bowl and lost 20-6. In our first 8 games of the season we won 7 and were headed for another great year. We were beaten badly by Pittsburgh on Monday Night Football with a 23-0 score. It was the first time we had been shutout in 133 games. O.J. Simpson and his offensive line called "The Electric Company" were honored at a dinner on the 20th anniversary of Simpson's 2,003-yard year. On December 26 we beat the Jets in the snow at home and clinched the AFC East title for the fifth time in six years. On January 15, one of the coldest days in Bills' history (0 degrees with a wind chill of minus 32), we defeated the Raiders 29-23, giving us the AFC Playoff victory. We then won the AFC Championship game vs. the Chiefs and became the first team in NFL history to reach the Super Bowl four straight years. We met the Cowboys in the Georgia Dome and once again we lost 30-13. The **coaster** started a downward turn.

Ralph Wilson watches at the Bills' summer camp at Fredonia State College.

1993

In a Sunday night game Kelly reorganizes his troops before beating the Giants 17-14.

Kenneth Davis #23 scores one of his two TDs that gave us the AFC East title over the Jets.

Another face on the sidelines that will be missed is security man Capt. Donald Kieffer of the Amherst Police Dept., who worked at the Bills games for Chase Security. Don was killed in a tragic parachute jumping accident in 1996.

Dan Marino #13 puts his arm around Nate Odomes #37 as Miami leaves the field with a victory.

1993

The 1973 offensive team poses for a reunion photo with O.J. to celebrate the 20th anniversary of his 2,003-yard season.

Elbert Dubenion (1960-68) has his name enshrined on the Wall of Fame in the stadium.

Thurman Thomas #34 looks as if he is about to go airborne vs. the Patriots.

SUPER BOWL XXVIII

VS. DALLAS COWBOYS • IN ATLANTA, GA • JANUARY 30, 1994
COWBOYS 30/ BILLS 13

We were unable to stop Emmitt Smith #22 of Dallas as he amassed 132 yards rushing.

Thurman Thomas #34 rushed for 37 yards.

1993

A prayer after the game is over. Bills lose 4th Super Bowl in a row.

For the first time in four years there was no Super Bowl trip for the Bills. After riding along the top of the **roller coaster** for four straight years, unable to grab the golden ring, we began a downward slide. We won 7 and lost 9 and failed to make the playoffs for the first time in six years. Our #1 draft choice this year was Jeff Burris of Notre Dame, and then we had three second-round choices, Bucky Brooks, Lonnie Johnson, and Sam Rogers. On the free agency market we lost two fine players including Nate Odomes and Pete Metzelaars. Construction began at the stadium and we added fourteen luxury suites with glassed-in club seating and the largest SONY JumboTron scoreboard in the United States. The year ended with the Bills out of contention and the **coaster ride** about to hit a curve with the loss of some big names in 1995.

New York Governor George Pataki gets a firsthand look at the Bills in action with Bill Munson (on right) of the Bills' staff.

1994

In a win over Miami. The Bills force a Miami fumble.

Don Beebe #82 waves to the crowd during a preseason game in Buffalo.

Left to right: Lou Piccone (1977-82), Ralph Wilson, and Ed Rutkowski (1963-68) talking over old times.

Ralph Wilson and Ed Abramoski, the trainer, watch the festivities.

On the field. Left to right: Bob Smith, photographer; Tom Day (1961-66); Dan Darragh (1968-70); Dick Cunningham (1967-72); and Jerry Butler (1979-83).

Even the Buffalo Jills had a reunion on the field as some of the former cheerleaders met again.

Left to right Paul Maguire 1964-70; Coach Lou Saban; and Ron McDole l963-70.

1994

Frank Reich #14 leads the Bills in a loss to the Vikings.

Butch Byrd (1964-70) is honored prior to the Chiefs vs. Bills game. We won 44-10.

Bruce Smith #78 causes a fumble by the Chiefs' QB Joe Montana #19.

This was the year that the Bills managed to get the **roller coaster** pulled up from the downward slide of 1994 with 10 wins and 6 losses and a place in the playoffs. We won the first playoff game against Miami, but when we played the Steelers in Pittsburgh we were soundly beaten 40-21. A bright item of the year was the acquisition of Bryce Paup from Green Bay through the free agency market. Paup was not only big in the Bills games, he won the title of NFL Defensive Player of the Year. Other players acquired by the Bills through the free agency market were Ted Washington and Jim Jeffcoat. The devastating news of the year was the loss of players due to the free agency market: Mike Lodish, Oliver Barnett, Darryl Talley, and Frank Reich would be greatly missed by teammates and fans. Don Beebe went with the Carolina Panthers. But we still managed to make the second round of the playoffs. The coaster has paused on the track, but it's still humming, ready for another climb toward the top. This book ends with the team ready, the coaches ready, the fans ready, and the photographers ready.

1995

A preseason game and the feelings along the sidelines are light. Left to right: Thurman Thomas #34, Carwell Garner #35, Bruce Smith #78, and Cornelius Bennett #97.

Thurman Thomas #34 holds up the ball after completing a 1,000-yard season.

Bryce Paup #95 became the NFL Defensive Player of the Year in 1995.

Bobby Chandler (Bills player 1971-79, deceased) would have been very proud to hear his 17 year-old daughter Marisa sing "The Star Spangled Banner" prior to the Colts game. Marisa has gone on to study at Harvard University.

Fans cheer after the Bills win AFC East.

An injured Andre Reed #83 watches the game from the stadium tunnel in Orchard Park, NY.

The leaders for TOMORROW: (Left to right) Quinn Early #88, Chris Spielman #54, Eric Moulds #80.

With Jim Kelly (center)..Quinn Early (left) and Eric Moulds.

Players line up to sign autographs at Mini Camp

1996

What will the year 1996 bring? Our **roller coaster** ride is over for now and we are poised waiting for the wheels to start moving upward. The leaders for 1996 are getting ready. Are You Ready? I AM...

PHOTOGRAPHER / AUTHOR

Robert L. Smith...your photographer.

Started as a professional photographer with Bell Aircraft for five years. Then went on to become a staff photographer for the *Buffalo Evening News (the Buffalo News)* from 1957-1995, when he retired with nearly forty years of service. He was the chief photographer of the Buffalo Bills from 1960 to the '90s. Part of his retirement project was to write this book and compile the photos of a lifetime. He is married to Jeanne and they have six children, Susan, Michael, Sandra, Robert Jr., Shawn, and Colleen. They also have seven grandchildren and live in Elma, New York.

CREDITS

Chet Kozlowski designed the book.
Carolyn McKibben was my copy editor.
Ralph Salerno coordinated the production of the book.
Keller Bros. & Miller Inc. in Buffalo, N.Y. did the printing.

DISTRIBUTION

Western New York Wares Inc.
P.O. Box 733 Ellicott Station
Buffalo, N.Y. 14205
Brian Meyer, Founder & President

THANKS

Thanks to **Eastman Kodak Co.** for supplying me the paper to print these photos.

All photographers have assistants, and my job with the Buffalo Bills brought in a few "special" folks that I would like to thank.

My four Number One assistants were **Fran Passuite,** a school teacher from Lockport, New York (now retired); **Susan Smith Mariacher,** a photographer and mother of three from Elma; **Robert Watroba,** a nature photographer also from Elma; and **Frank Woods** of Springbrook, my right hand man since the early years.

Additional photographers that I would like to thank for being there when needed are: Jack Stanley, Jim McCoy, Bob Kirkham, Dr. Tony Russo, Robert Stoddard, Jon Cylka, Jim Warder, Ed Sullivan, Robert L. Smith Jr., Bob Bukaty, Peter Barber, Colleen Fintak Vigneron, Rob McElroy, Bruce Anderson, Ronald R. Smith, David Mariacher, Sandi Smith, Mike Fintak, Lois Bernstein, John Russell, Mike Groll, Bill Wippert, and Raymond "Tex" Smith, my Dad.

I would like to say a special thanks to my wife, Jeanne, who has put up with my daily routine of searching for the best of the best for this book. Also for her help in editing these many pages and the giving of her time so I could search through thirty-six years of negatives and prints.

Thank you, one and all. This book is a part of all of us.